Mastering ISO/IEC 20000-1

By Kris Hermans

Disclaimer

Copyright © the Year 2023

All Rights Reserved.

No part of this eBook can be transmitted or reproduced in any form, including print, electronic, photocopying, scanning, mechanical, or recording, without prior written permission from the author.

While the author has made utmost efforts to ensure the accuracy of the written content, all readers are advised to follow the information mentioned herein at their own risk. The author cannot be held responsible for any personal or commercial damage caused by misinterpretation of information. All readers are encouraged to seek professional advice when needed.

This ebook has been written for information purposes only. Every effort has been made to make this eBook as complete and accurate as possible. However, there may be mistakes in typography or content. Also, this e-book provides information only up to the publishing date. Therefore, this eBook should be used as a guide - not as the ultimate source.

The purpose of this eBook is to educate. The author and the publisher do not warrant that the information contained in this ebook is fully complete and shall not be responsible for any errors or omissions. The author and publisher shall have neither liability nor responsibility to any person or entity with respect to any loss or damage caused or alleged to be caused directly or indirectly by this e-book.

Table of Contents

Chapter 1: Introduction to ISO/IEC 20000-1 1
   1.1 The Evolution of IT Service Management 2
   1.2 The Purpose & Benefits of ISO/IEC 20000-1 5
   1.3 Understanding the ISO/IEC 20000 Family of Standards 7
   1.4 Key Concepts and Terminology 10

Chapter 2: Scope and Requirements of ISO/IEC 20000-1 12
   2.1 Defining the Scope of the Standard 13
   2.2 Understanding the Requirements of ISO/IEC 20000-1 15
   2.3 Compliance and Certification Processes 18
      Compliance Process 18
      Certification Process 19
   2.4 Mapping ISO/IEC 20000-1 with Other Frameworks (ITIL, COBIT, etc.) 20
      Mapping with ITIL 21
      Mapping with COBIT 21
      Mapping with Other Frameworks 22

Chapter 3: Service Management System (SMS) 23
   3.1 Designing and Implementing an Effective SMS 24
      Defining the Scope of the SMS 24
      Establishing the SMS Policy 24
      Planning the SMS 24
      Implementing the SMS 25
      Documentation 25
      Performance Evaluation 26
      Continual Improvement 26
   3.2 Defining Policies, Objectives, and Processes 26
      Defining Policies 27
      Defining Objectives 27
      Establishing Processes 28
   3.3 Roles and Responsibilities in the SMS 28
      Top Management 29
      Service Management System Manager 29

- Process Owners 30
- Service Owners 30
- Other Roles 30
- 3.4 Continual Improvement and Performance Monitoring 31
  - Continual Improvement 31
  - Performance Monitoring 32
- Chapter 4: Planning and Implementing Service Management Processes 34
  - 4.1 Service Strategy and Design Processes 35
    - Service Strategy 35
    - Service Design 36
  - 4.2 Service Transition and Service Operation Processes 37
    - Service Transition 37
    - Service Operation 38
  - 4.3 Incident Management and Problem Management 39
    - Incident Management 40
    - Problem Management 40
    - The Interrelation of Incident and Problem Management 41
  - 4.4 Change Management and Configuration Management 42
    - Change Management 42
    - Configuration Management 43
    - Interrelation of Change and Configuration Management 44
  - 4.5 Release and Deployment Management 45
    - Release Management 45
    - Deployment Management 46
    - The Interrelation of Release and Deployment Management 47
  - 4.6 Service Level Management and Service Reporting 47
    - Service Level Management 47
    - Service Reporting 48
    - Interrelation of Service Level Management and Service Reporting 49
  - 4.7 Service Continuity and Availability Management 49
    - Service Continuity Management 50
    - Availability Management 51
    - Interrelation of Service Continuity and Availability Management 51
  - 4.8 Supplier Management and Relationship Management 52
    - Supplier Management 52

- Relationship Management 53
  - Interrelation of Supplier Management and Relationship Management 54
- Chapter 5: Service Measurement and Reporting 56
  - 5.1 Defining Key Performance Indicators (KPIs) 57
    - The Role of KPIs in ITSM 58
    - Defining Effective KPIs 58
    - Examples of KPIs in ITSM 59
  - 5.2 Data Collection, Analysis, and Reporting 60
    - Data Collection 60
    - Data Analysis 61
    - Data Reporting 62
  - 5.3 Service Reporting and Communication 62
    - Service Reporting 63
    - Service Communication 63
  - 5.4 Benchmarking and Best Practices 65
    - Benchmarking 65
    - Best Practices 66
- Chapter 6: Service Improvement and Continual Service Improvement (CSI) 68
  - 6.1 The Importance of Service Improvement 69
    - Ensuring Customer Satisfaction and Loyalty 69
    - Maintaining Relevance in a Competitive Market 70
    - Efficiency and Productivity Improvements 70
    - Risk Management 71
    - Achieving Business Objectives 71
  - 6.2 Implementing a CSI Process 71
    - Understanding the Continual Service Improvement Process 72
    - Establishing a Continual Service Improvement Process 72
    - Cultural Considerations 74
  - 6.3 Root Cause Analysis and Problem-Solving Techniques 74
    - Root Cause Analysis 75
    - The Role of RCA and Problem-Solving in ITSM 76
  - 6.4 Implementing Service Improvement Initiatives 77
    - Recognizing the Need for Service Improvement 77
    - Planning the Service Improvement Initiative 77
    - Defining Metrics and KPIs 78

- Implementing the Initiative 78
- Monitoring and Review 78
- Challenges and Best Practices 79

Chapter 7: People, Competence, and Training 80

7.1 Human Resource Management in IT Service Management 81
- Recruitment and Selection 81
- Training and Development 81
- Performance Management 82
- Employee Engagement and Retention 82
- Compliance with ISO/IEC 20000-1 83

7.2 Competence Framework and Skills Development 83
- The Role of a Competence Framework 83
- Frameworks for Competence in ITSM 84
- Skills Development in ITSM 85
- Aligning with ISO/IEC 20000-1 Requirements 85

7.3 Training and Development Programs 86
- Importance of Training and Development in ITSM 86
- Designing Effective Training and Development Programs 87
- Assessing and Enhancing Training Effectiveness 87
- Training and Development as an Ongoing Commitment 88

7.4 Motivation, Engagement, and Performance Management 88
- Motivation in ITSM 89
- Engagement in ITSM 89
- Performance Management in ITSM 90
- Integrating Motivation, Engagement, and Performance Management in ITSM 90

Chapter 8: Technology and Tooling for Service Management 92
- 8.1 Service Management Tools and Automation 93
- 8.2 Configuration Management Databases (CMDBs) 95
- 8.3 Incident and Problem Management Tools 97
- 8.4 Change and Release Management Tools 99
- 8.5 Performance Monitoring and Reporting Tools 101

Chapter 9: Service Integration and Management (SIAM) 104
- 9.1 Understanding SIAM Principles and Concepts 105
- 9.2 Implementing SIAM in a Multi-sourced Environment 107
  - Initial Assessment: 107

Mastering ISO/IEC 20000-1

- Designing the SIAM Model: 107
- Implementation and Transition: 108
- Service Integration: 108
- Performance Monitoring and Continual Improvement: 108
- 9.3 SIAM Governance and Integration Models 109
  - SIAM Governance 110
  - SIAM Integration Models 111
- 9.4 Challenges and Best Practices in SIAM Implementation 112
  - Challenges in SIAM Implementation 112
  - Best Practices in SIAM Implementation 113
- Chapter 10: Service Management and Business Relationship Management 115
  - 10.1 Aligning IT Services with Business Objectives 116
  - 10.2 Building Effective Relationships with Business Stakeholders 118
  - 10.3 Customer Satisfaction and Service Experience Management 120
  - 10.4 Business-IT Alignment and Value Creation 123
- Chapter 11: Auditing, Compliance, and Certification 126
  - 11.1 Internal Audits and Self-Assessment 126
  - 11.2 Preparing for External Audits 128
  - 11.3 Achieving ISO/IEC 20000-1 Certification 131
    - Step 1: Initial Assessment and Gap Analysis 131
    - Step 2: Obtain Management Commitment 131
    - Step 3: Develop an Implementation Plan 131
    - Step 4: Train and Educate Staff 132
    - Step 5: Develop and Implement Processes 132
    - Step 6: Monitor and Measure 132
    - Step 7: Internal Audit 133
    - Step 8: Management Review 133
    - Step 9: External Audit 133
    - Step 10: Certification and Continual Improvement 133
  - 11.4 Sustaining Compliance and Continual Improvement 134
    - Sustaining Compliance 134
    - Continual Improvement 135
- Chapter 12: Emerging Trends and Future of IT Service Management 137
  - 12.1 The Impact of Digital Transformation on ITSM 137
  - 12.2 Agile and DevOps in Service Management 139

12.3 Cloud Computing and IT Service Delivery 141
12.4 Artificial Intelligence and Automation in ITSM 144
Appendix 147
ISO/IEC 20000-1:2018 Standard at a Glance 147
Sample Templates and Checklists for ISO/IEC 20000-1 Implementation 149
Case Studies and Success Stories 151
Case Study 1: A Large Financial Institution 152
Case Study 2: A Global Software Company 152
Glossary of Key Terms and Acronyms 153
About the author 157

Chapter 1: Introduction to ISO/IEC 20000-1

Welcome to the world of IT Service Management and ISO/IEC 20000-1, the international standard for IT Service Management. As technology continues to evolve and integrate more deeply into business operations, the importance of having a robust and effective IT Service Management system is more crucial than ever. In this first chapter, we will introduce you to the ISO/IEC 20000-1 standard, providing a thorough overview to help you understand its importance and relevance in today's technology-driven business environment.

This chapter begins with a historical look at the evolution of IT Service Management, tracing its roots, its development, and the challenges and changes that led to the creation of structured methodologies and standards. Understanding this history will give you a sense of why ISO/IEC 20000-1 exists and how it fits into the broader IT landscape.

We will then delve into the purpose and benefits of ISO/IEC 20000-1, highlighting why businesses and organizations globally adopt it. The standard is not just a guide but a tool that organizations can use to ensure that their IT services align with their business needs, delivering value and efficiency. We will explore these benefits in-depth, providing examples and scenarios that highlight the impact of ISO/IEC 20000-1 implementation.

To give you a more comprehensive understanding, we will also introduce you to the ISO/IEC 20000 family of standards. This family is like a toolkit that businesses can use to address different aspects of IT service management, from service delivery and reporting to disaster recovery.

Finally, we will cover key concepts and terminology that will serve as a foundation for the rest of the book. Like learning any new language, grasping these terms is crucial to understanding and implementing the standard.

This chapter lays the groundwork for our journey into ISO/IEC 20000-1. It is designed to give you a solid understanding of what the standard is, why it is important, and how it fits into the larger picture of IT service management. Whether you are a professional looking to implement the standard in your organization, an auditor tasked with assessing compliance, or a student of IT service management, this chapter provides the knowledge and context you need to navigate the landscape of ISO/IEC 20000-1.

1.1 The Evolution of IT Service Management

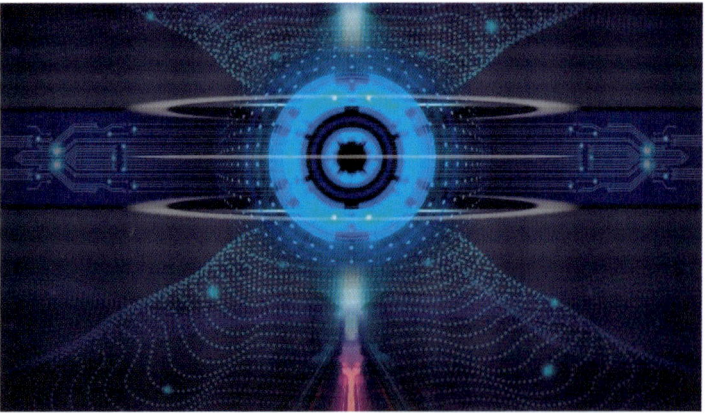

The evolution of IT Service Management (ITSM) is a fascinating journey that reflects the rapid advancements and changes in technology. It's a tale that mirrors the shift from mere operational IT to strategic IT that aligns with business goals and customer expectations. This transformation didn't happen overnight. Instead, it evolved through several key phases and was influenced by different methodologies and standards, such as the ISO/IEC 20000-1.

In the early days of computing, during the 1960s and 70s, the focus of IT was primarily on the development and operation of mainframe systems. At that time, the primary concern was to make systems work and fix them when they broke. However, as technology grew more complex and organizations began to rely more heavily on IT for their operations, the need for structured processes and practices to manage these systems became clear.

In the 1980s, as technology started becoming an integral part of business operations, organizations began to recognize the need for a more strategic approach to managing their IT systems. This need gave birth to the concept of IT Service Management. During this era, IT departments transitioned from being simply a support function to becoming strategic partners that could provide value to the business. The goal of ITSM was to ensure that IT services were delivered in a way that aligned with business needs.

In the late 1980s and early 1990s, ITIL (Information Technology Infrastructure Library) was developed by the UK government's Central Computer and Telecommunications Agency (CCTA). It was an attempt to standardize the hitherto ad hoc and disjointed practices in IT service management. ITIL provided a set of best-practice publications for ITSM that focused on aligning IT services with the needs of business. The widespread adoption of ITIL marked a significant turning point in the history of ITSM, putting structure and standardization into the process of managing IT services.

As organizations entered the new millennium, the need for more robust and reliable IT services became even more pronounced. The rise of e-commerce and digital business models led to an increased reliance on IT systems, making effective ITSM crucial for business success. Recognizing this, the International Organization for Standardization (ISO) and the International Electrotechnical Commission (IEC) developed ISO/IEC 20000, the first international standard for IT service management. First published in 2005, ISO/IEC 20000 provided a set of standardized requirements for an IT service management system (SMS).

The creation of ISO/IEC 20000 represented a significant advancement in the field of ITSM. For the first time, there was a globally recognized standard that organizations could follow to ensure their ITSM processes were robust and effective. ISO/IEC 20000-1, part of this series, sets the requirements for the service management system, and it has been widely adopted by organizations seeking to improve their ITSM and demonstrate their capabilities to customers, partners, and regulators.

The most recent iteration, ISO/IEC 20000-1:2018, has been updated to respond to the ever-changing service management landscape, with its growing reliance on cloud services, digital transformation, and agile methods. It places a stronger emphasis on the integration and coordination of activities and on the utilization of assets and resources, marking a shift from a process-based approach to a more holistic management system view.

Today, as we stand in the age of digital transformation, artificial intelligence, and cloud computing, ITSM has become more vital than ever. It's no longer just about supporting business operations; it's about enabling business strategy and providing a competitive edge. In this era, ITSM means ensuring that technology not only supports but enables business objectives and that it can adapt rapidly to changing business needs.

Looking back, we can see how ITSM has evolved from a basic operational function to a strategic element of business success. Its evolution reflects the changing role of technology within businesses and the growing recognition of the importance of structured, strategic management of IT services. As we move forward, the evolution of ITSM is set to continue, adapting and changing to meet the demands of an increasingly digital, interconnected, and fast-paced business landscape.

IT Service Management has come a long way since its inception, and it continues to evolve, embracing newer technologies and methodologies. The journey has seen the rise of standards like ISO/IEC 20000-1 that provide organizations with clear guidelines and frameworks for managing their IT services. As we look ahead, the evolution of ITSM is likely to continue to be shaped by advances in technology and changes in the way businesses operate, ensuring that ITSM remains a dynamic and essential field.

1.2 The Purpose & Benefits of ISO/IEC 20000-1

ISO/IEC 20000-1 is the international standard that provides a set of standardized requirements for an effective IT service management system (SMS). Its main purpose is to help organizations establish and improve their ITSM practices by implementing an integrated system of processes and procedures designed to deliver effective IT services that support business objectives. But why has it become such an important framework for many organizations worldwide? In this section, we'll delve into the purpose and benefits of ISO/IEC 20000-1 and examine how it contributes to business success.

The primary purpose of ISO/IEC 20000-1 is to provide a framework for managing the service lifecycle effectively. This includes the design, transition, delivery, and improvement of services that fulfill service requirements and provide value to both customers and service providers. The standard sets a high level of quality for service management processes, enabling organizations to demonstrate service excellence and win the trust of customers, stakeholders, and partners.

One of the significant benefits of ISO/IEC 20000-1 is that it enables organizations to align their IT services with their business needs. This alignment is crucial because, in today's digital age, IT services often play a significant role in an organization's operations and strategic goals. By implementing an SMS that aligns with ISO/IEC 20000-1, organizations can ensure their IT services support their business objectives effectively and efficiently.

ISO/IEC 20000-1 also provides a framework for continuous improvement. By setting out clear requirements for the establishment, implementation, maintenance, and continual improvement of an SMS, the standard encourages organizations to continually monitor, review, and improve their service management practices. This focus on continuous improvement can help organizations become more efficient, reduce costs, and enhance service quality over time.

Another significant benefit of ISO/IEC 20000-1 is that it helps to establish clear roles and responsibilities for service management processes. This clarity can enhance collaboration and communication within the organization, leading to more efficient service delivery and fewer misunderstandings or conflicts.

Furthermore, achieving ISO/IEC 20000-1 certification can enhance an organization's reputation. It sends a clear message to customers, partners, and stakeholders that the organization is committed to service excellence and has the processes and systems in place to deliver it. This can help to build trust, improve customer satisfaction, and provide a competitive advantage in the marketplace.

On a practical level, ISO/IEC 20000-1 also provides a toolkit for managing risk and maintaining resilience. By requiring organizations to establish processes for incident and problem management, change management, and continuity and availability management, the standard helps them to identify, manage, and reduce risks related to their IT services. This can enhance the organization's resilience and its ability to respond effectively to changes, disruptions, and challenges.

The benefits of ISO/IEC 20000-1 extend beyond the organization itself. For customers, the standard provides assurance that the organization is capable of delivering consistent, reliable, and high-quality IT services. This can improve customer satisfaction and enhance the customer's trust in the organization.

For regulators and auditors, ISO/IEC 20000-1 provides a recognized benchmark against which to assess the organization's service management practices. This can simplify regulatory compliance and auditing processes and provide transparency and assurance about the organization's capabilities.

For employees, working in an organization that aligns with ISO/IEC 20000-1 can offer benefits such as clearer roles and responsibilities, better communication, and opportunities for professional development. The standard's emphasis on continual improvement can contribute to a positive work culture that values learning and improvement.

In conclusion, ISO/IEC 20000-1 serves a dual purpose. On the one hand, it helps organizations improve their ITSM practices, align their IT services with business objectives, manage risk, and demonstrate their commitment to service excellence. On the other hand, it benefits customers, regulators, and employees by providing assurance about the organization's service management capabilities, simplifying compliance and auditing, and contributing to a positive work culture. By achieving ISO/IEC 20000-1 certification, organizations can unlock these benefits and enhance their success in today's digital, interconnected business landscape.

1.3 Understanding the ISO/IEC 20000 Family of Standards

ISO/IEC 20000 is a family of international standards that set the globally accepted best practices for IT Service Management. Developed by the International Organization for Standardization (ISO) and the International Electrotechnical Commission (IEC), this family of standards aims to help organizations ensure they have robust, reliable IT services that support their business objectives. The ISO/IEC 20000 family consists of several parts, each addressing different aspects of IT Service Management. To understand the scope and application of these standards, it is essential to familiarize oneself with each part.

ISO/IEC 20000-1 is the core standard in this series and the focus of our discussion in this book. As mentioned earlier, it provides the requirements for a service management system (SMS). This includes the planning, design, transition, delivery, and improvement of IT services. It also lays down requirements for establishing policies, objectives, and processes that facilitate the delivery of high-quality IT services. Moreover, it promotes the alignment of IT services with business needs, enhancing overall organizational performance.

ISO/IEC 20000-2 provides guidance on the application of service management systems. It complements ISO/IEC 20000-1 by providing practical advice on how to implement an SMS. It offers explanations, recommendations, and examples to assist organizations in understanding and applying the requirements of ISO/IEC 20000-1. Although it's not a requirement for certification, it can be immensely useful for those implementing or improving their SMS.

ISO/IEC 20000-3 provides guidance on the scope definition and applicability of ISO/IEC 20000-1. It aids organizations in assessing whether ISO/IEC 20000-1 is relevant and applicable to them. This part also provides guidance on how to define the scope of an SMS, which can be especially useful for large organizations or those with complex IT infrastructures.

ISO/IEC 20000-10 describes the core concepts of the ISO/IEC 20000 series and its terms and definitions. It also provides an overview of the other parts of the ISO/IEC 20000 series. This document is useful for anyone wanting to understand the ISO/IEC 20000 series better, including top management, IT staff, and auditors.

The other parts of the ISO/IEC 20000 series provide specific guidance on different aspects of service management, such as service reporting (ISO/IEC 20000-7), service catalog management (ISO/IEC 20000-15), and asset and configuration management (ISO/IEC 20000-20). These parts are not mandatory for certification but can provide valuable guidance for organizations seeking to implement specific ITSM processes or improve certain aspects of their service management.

Understanding the ISO/IEC 20000 family of standards and their interrelationships can help organizations gain a holistic view of IT Service Management. Each part of the series has a distinct role to play, and together they provide a comprehensive framework for implementing effective ITSM practices.

The benefits of adopting the ISO/IEC 20000 family of standards are manifold. Firstly, they promote the alignment of IT services with business needs, which can enhance the efficiency and effectiveness of IT service delivery. Secondly, they provide a framework for continuous improvement, encouraging organizations to review and improve their ITSM practices regularly. Thirdly, they provide clear benchmarks against which organizations can assess their performance and demonstrate their service management capabilities to customers, partners, and regulators.

Adopting the ISO/IEC 20000 standards also facilitates risk management. By requiring organizations to establish processes for risk identification and mitigation, these standards help organizations manage risks related to their IT services more effectively. Furthermore, these standards can aid regulatory compliance by providing a recognized benchmark against which to assess ITSM practices.

In conclusion, the ISO/IEC 20000 family of standards provides a comprehensive framework for managing IT services effectively. By understanding these standards and applying them in their ITSM practices, organizations can enhance their service delivery, manage risk, and demonstrate their commitment to service excellence. The journey to understanding and implementing these standards may be challenging, but the benefits they bring can make it a rewarding one.

1.4 Key Concepts and Terminology

In order to fully grasp the requirements and implications of the ISO/IEC 20000-1 standard, it's crucial to understand the key concepts and terminology used within it. This common language enables clear communication and understanding across different stakeholders, making it easier to implement, maintain, and improve an IT service management system (SMS).

Service Management System (SMS): At the heart of the ISO/IEC 20000-1 standard is the SMS, which is the overarching management system used to establish, implement, operate, monitor, review, maintain, and improve service management. It encompasses the policies, objectives, plans, procedures, processes, and resources required to manage services.

Services and Service Management: Services in this context refer to the means of delivering value to customers by achieving their desired results without the ownership of specific costs and risks. Service management is a set of specialized capabilities for delivering value to customers in the form of services.

Service Provider: A service provider is an organization delivering services to customers. A service provider could be an internal organization providing IT services to the rest of the business, or it could be a company providing IT services to external customers.

Customers and Users: In the ISO/IEC 20000-1 standard, a customer is defined as the person or group that commissions and usually funds the service, often through a service level agreement (SLA). A user, on the other hand, is the person or group that uses the service. Users are often the customers, but not always.

Service Lifecycle: The service lifecycle concept encompasses all stages of a service from its initial design and implementation through to its eventual retirement. The lifecycle typically includes stages such as service design, transition, operation, and continual improvement.

Service Requirements: These are the requirements for a service as agreed between a service provider and a customer. They are usually documented in a service level agreement (SLA).

Service Level Agreement (SLA): An SLA is a documented agreement between a service provider and a customer that specifies services to be provided, their expected levels of performance, and the responsibilities of both parties.

Process: A process is a set of interrelated or interacting activities which transforms inputs into outputs. In the context of an SMS, these processes are often ITIL-aligned processes, such as incident management, change management, and configuration management.

Procedure: A procedure is a specified way to carry out an activity or a process. Procedures are more detailed than processes and describe who does what, when they do it, and under what criteria.

Policy: A policy is a formally documented management intent to direct and control an organization's actions in a particular area. Policies usually outline a set of rules or principles that guide decisions and achieve rational outcomes.

Objective: An objective is a result to be achieved. In the context of ISO/IEC 20000-1, objectives are typically aligned with business objectives and the improvement of service management.

Understanding these key concepts and terminology is fundamental to implementing and maintaining an SMS in line with ISO/IEC 20000-1. It ensures that all stakeholders, from service providers and customers to auditors and employees, are speaking the same language, thereby facilitating more effective communication, cooperation, and coordination. With a solid understanding of these foundational terms and concepts, organizations can set the stage for more effective and efficient implementation of ISO/IEC 20000-1 and, ultimately, the delivery of higher-quality services.

Chapter 2: Scope and Requirements of ISO/IEC 20000-1

As we delve deeper into the realm of ISO/IEC 20000-1, we come to an aspect that demands a comprehensive understanding for successful application - the Scope and Requirements of ISO/IEC 20000-1. This chapter aims to enlighten you about the scope of the standard and its numerous requirements, which form the backbone of any IT Service Management System (SMS) aspiring to gain ISO/IEC 20000-1 certification.

The section on defining the scope of the standard will elucidate what aspects of an organization's IT service management the standard applies, the kind of organizations for which the standard is intended, and what services are encompassed within its purview. Clear demarcation of the scope ensures that the implementation of the standard is focused, effective, and consistent with the organization's business objectives.

Understanding the requirements of ISO/IEC 20000-1 forms a significant part of this chapter. The standard's requirements pertain to various facets of an IT service management system, from the design, transition, delivery, and control of services to the continual improvement of these services and the system as a whole. This section will guide you through these requirements, providing an in-depth look into each one.

Furthermore, the chapter will address compliance and certification processes. It will highlight the importance of adhering to the standard's requirements, explain the implications of non-compliance, and take you through the certification process.

Finally, the chapter will present a discussion on mapping ISO/IEC 20000-1 with other frameworks like ITIL, COBIT, and more. This will illuminate how ISO/IEC 20000-1 can be aligned and integrated with these other well-known frameworks, thus enhancing its effectiveness and utility for the organization.

By the end of this chapter, you will have gained a robust understanding of the ISO/IEC 20000-1's scope and requirements and how to apply this knowledge to your organization's advantage. Let's begin this insightful journey.

2.1 Defining the Scope of the Standard

ISO/IEC 20000-1 is the international standard for service management, applicable to any organization, regardless of its size, type, or the nature of the services it provides. The primary aim of the standard is to establish a framework for an organization to effectively deliver managed services that meet business and customer requirements.

The first step towards implementing ISO/IEC 20000-1 is defining the scope of the standard within the organization's context. The scope outlines the boundaries of the service management system (SMS), clearly stating what parts of the organization, which services, and which locations will be covered by the system. Defining the scope is a critical process as it delineates where the standard will be applied and sets the stage for the implementation of the SMS.

While the ISO/IEC 20000-1 standard can be applied to any organization, it is particularly relevant for organizations that have a strong reliance on IT services, such as IT service providers, IT departments in organizations, IT outsourcing companies, and businesses heavily dependent on IT systems for their operations. The standard is also relevant for organizations that need to demonstrate their capability to provide reliable and quality services, either to meet regulatory requirements or to enhance customer confidence and satisfaction.

When defining the scope, several key factors need to be considered:

1. Services: Clearly define the services that will be covered by the SMS. These could range from IT support services, software development, IT infrastructure management, cloud services, and data center services to any other IT services that the organization provides. The services included in the scope should be those where the organization has control over the service provision.

2. Locations: Determine the geographical locations that will be included in the scope of the SMS. This could be a single location, multiple locations, or all locations, depending on the organization's structure and where it delivers its services.

3. Organizational Units: Identify the departments, teams, or business units that will be involved in the delivery of the services included in the scope. This could include the IT department, customer service teams, and any other unit that plays a role in service provision.

4. Processes: Specify the processes that will be part of the SMS. These could include all processes required by the ISO/IEC 20000-1 standard, such as service delivery processes, relationship processes, resolution processes, control processes, and any other processes that the organization has in place for service management.

The scope should be documented and should clearly communicate to all relevant parties what parts of the organization and which services are covered by the SMS. This document should be readily available and easily understood by everyone within the organization.

Moreover, when defining the scope, it is crucial to ensure that it aligns with the organization's business objectives. The SMS should support the business's strategic direction, and the scope should reflect this alignment. Additionally, the defined scope should be realistic and manageable, considering the organization's resources and capabilities.

ISO/IEC 20000-1 also emphasizes the concept of a service management system's continual improvement. Therefore, the scope does not have to cover all services, processes, and locations at the outset. An organization can start with a more limited scope and expand it gradually over time as the SMS matures and the organization's capability to manage more services and processes improves.

Defining the scope is not a one-time activity but should be revisited regularly as the organization evolves, new services are added, or existing services are modified or retired. Changes in the business environment, regulatory requirements, technology advancements, or customer expectations may also necessitate a revision of the scope.

In conclusion, defining the scope of the ISO/IEC 20000-1 standard is a crucial starting point in the implementation of an effective service management system. It helps the organization focus its efforts on areas that are most relevant and beneficial. While it can be a challenging task, a well-defined scope is instrumental in the successful implementation and certification of an SMS. It provides clarity, direction and sets the foundation for a service management system that delivers value to the business and its customers.

2.2 Understanding the Requirements of ISO/IEC 20000-1

The ISO/IEC 20000-1 standard sets out a comprehensive set of requirements for an effective IT service management system (SMS). These requirements are aimed at establishing a systematic approach to planning, establishing, implementing, operating, monitoring, reviewing, maintaining, and improving an SMS. They encompass a broad array of elements such as policies, plans, objectives, processes, people, and resources. Understanding these requirements is fundamental to aligning IT services with the needs of the business and the expectations of the customers.

The requirements of ISO/IEC 20000-1 are categorized into several sections, each of which focuses on a specific aspect of service management. This is designed to ensure a holistic approach to the management of services, considering all the aspects that contribute to effective service management.

1. Service Management System General Requirements: These requirements are the backbone of the standard, laying down the basic principles for designing, implementing, and maintaining an SMS. It includes establishing and improving the SMS, documentation requirements, resource management, and establishing and managing the scope and boundaries of the SMS.

2. Design and Transition of New or Changed Services: This section details the requirements for the design, transition, and delivery of services. It emphasizes the importance of adequately designing and transitioning services to ensure they meet customer requirements and are effectively integrated into the service environment.

3. Service Delivery Processes: This covers the requirements for the delivery of services, focusing on aspects such as service level management, service reporting, capacity management, service continuity and availability management, budgeting and accounting for services, and information security management. The requirements in this section are centered around ensuring that services are delivered at agreed-upon levels, are reliable and secure, and that their performance is regularly reported and reviewed.

4. Relationship Processes: This section lays out the requirements for the management of relationships with customers and suppliers. This includes requirements for the identification of customer requirements, the handling of customer complaints, and the management of relationships with suppliers to ensure they contribute effectively to service delivery.

5. Resolution Processes: These requirements deal with the resolution of incidents and problems. They include requirements for incident and problem management, ensuring that disruptions to services are minimized and that the root causes of incidents are identified and addressed to prevent recurrence.

6. Control Processes: This section details the requirements for the control of the organization's assets and resources. It includes requirements for configuration management and change management, aimed at ensuring that all assets are adequately controlled and that all changes are managed in a systematic manner to minimize the impact on services.

The requirements of ISO/IEC 20000-1 are designed to be applicable to all types of organizations, regardless of their size, type, or the nature of the services they provide. However, the way in which these requirements are implemented can vary significantly depending on the context of the organization, its specific objectives, the complexity of its services, and its operating environment.

Moreover, it's important to note that the ISO/IEC 20000-1 requirements are focused on the management system for services, rather than the specific technical competencies or the details of how the services are delivered. The emphasis is on establishing a robust system for managing services that can be adapted and improved over time to meet changing business needs and customer expectations.

By comprehending these requirements, organizations can establish a comprehensive framework for service management that enhances the quality and reliability of their services, improves customer satisfaction, and contributes to the achievement of their business objectives. Understanding these requirements is the first step in this journey, setting the groundwork for the effective implementation of an SMS in line with the ISO/IEC 20000-1 standard.

2.3 Compliance and Certification Processes

Compliance with ISO/IEC 20000-1 and the associated certification process signifies an organization's commitment to efficient and effective IT Service Management (ITSM). It provides external validation of an organization's ability to consistently deliver high-quality IT services that meet both customer needs and statutory and regulatory requirements.

Compliance Process
The first step towards achieving compliance with ISO/IEC 20000-1 is gaining a thorough understanding of the standard's requirements, which we discussed in the previous section. The next steps are the planning and implementation phases. This involves developing a

detailed plan outlining how the organization intends to meet each of the standard's requirements and then putting this plan into action.

Once the Service Management System (SMS) has been implemented, the organization needs to carry out regular internal audits to verify conformity with the standard's requirements and to assess the effectiveness of the SMS. Non-conformities identified during these audits need to be addressed through corrective actions.

In addition to internal audits, management reviews should be conducted at planned intervals to ensure the SMS's continuing suitability, adequacy, and effectiveness. Management reviews should address the possible need for changes to policy, objectives, targets, and other elements of the SMS. The outputs from management reviews should include decisions and actions related to possible changes to the SMS, improvements to the service management processes, and resource needs.

Certification Process

The certification process for ISO/IEC 20000-1 involves a two-stage audit conducted by an accredited certification body. The aim of this process is to verify that the organization's SMS conforms to the requirements of the standard and that it is effectively implemented and maintained.

1. **Stage 1 Audit (Readiness Review):** This preliminary audit assesses the readiness of the organization to move forward to the stage 2 audit. The auditor will review the organization's SMS documentation, including the service management policy, objectives, procedures, and records. The auditor will also evaluate the organization's understanding of the standard's requirements, the scope of the SMS, and the status of implementation.

2. **Stage 2 Audit (Certification Audit):** The stage 2 audit is a more detailed and thorough examination of the SMS. The auditor will examine the effectiveness of the SMS and the organization's

compliance with all the requirements of the ISO/IEC 20000-1 standard. This involves a review of records, interviews with staff, and observation of work activities and processes.

If any non-conformities are identified during the stage 2 audit, the organization will need to take corrective action to address these before certification can be awarded. Once the certification body is satisfied that the organization complies with all the requirements of the standard, it will issue an ISO/IEC 20000-1 certification.

The ISO/IEC 20000-1 certificate is valid for three years. However, the certification body will conduct surveillance audits, typically annually, to ensure that the SMS continues to conform to the standard and that continual improvement is being maintained.

In conclusion, achieving compliance with ISO/IEC 20000-1 and obtaining certification is a significant undertaking that requires a strong commitment from the entire organization, particularly top management. However, the benefits of improved service quality, increased customer satisfaction, and enhanced reputation can make this effort worthwhile. Furthermore, the process of implementing the standard's requirements can provide valuable insights into the organization's operations and identify opportunities for improvement.

2.4 Mapping ISO/IEC 20000-1 with Other Frameworks (ITIL, COBIT, etc.)

Understanding the relationship between ISO/IEC 20000-1 and other frameworks such as ITIL, COBIT, and others can be instrumental for organizations looking to leverage multiple approaches to improve their IT service management. Each of these frameworks provides unique perspectives and methodologies for managing IT services, and they can be used in conjunction with ISO/IEC 20000-1 to create a robust, holistic IT service management system (SMS).

Mapping with ITIL

ITIL (Information Technology Infrastructure Library) is one of the most widely used frameworks for IT service management. The ITIL framework provides a set of best practices for the delivery and management of IT services, with a focus on aligning IT services with the needs of the business.

ISO/IEC 20000-1 and ITIL have a close relationship, as the former is, in many ways, a formalization of the practices and principles found in ITIL. Both share a similar philosophy of continual improvement, and many of the processes described in ITIL can be mapped directly to the requirements of ISO/IEC 20000-1.

For instance, ITIL's service strategy, design, transition, operation, and continual service improvement lifecycle stages align well with ISO/IEC 20000-1's requirements for service delivery processes, relationship processes, resolution processes, control processes, and continual improvement. Organizations that have implemented ITIL will often find it easier to achieve ISO/IEC 20000-1 certification, as they are likely to already have many of the necessary practices and processes in place.

However, it's important to note that while ITIL is a set of best practices, ISO/IEC 20000-1 is a standard. This means that ISO/IEC 20000-1 provides specific requirements for what organizations must do, while ITIL offers guidance on how to do it. Therefore, while they complement each other, they have different roles in the IT service management landscape.

Mapping with COBIT

COBIT (Control Objectives for Information and Related Technologies) is a framework for the governance and management of enterprise IT. It provides a set of control objectives to help organizations meet business objectives through effective IT management.

While ISO/IEC 20000-1 focuses primarily on the management of IT services, COBIT has a broader scope, looking at the overall governance and management of IT at an enterprise level. This includes areas such as risk management, information security management, and enterprise architecture.

Despite their different focuses, there is considerable overlap between COBIT and ISO/IEC 20000-1. For instance, the COBIT domains of Align, Plan, and Organize (APO), and Build, Acquire and Implement (BAI) contain control objectives that can be mapped to the service management system requirements and the service delivery processes of ISO/IEC 20000-1.

By using COBIT in conjunction with ISO/IEC 20000-1, organizations can ensure that their IT services are not only managed effectively but are also aligned with their business objectives and governed according to best practices.

Mapping with Other Frameworks
In addition to ITIL and COBIT, there are other frameworks and standards that can be used in conjunction with ISO/IEC 20000-1. For example, the ISO/IEC 27001 standard for information security management can be integrated with ISO/IEC 20000-1 to ensure that IT services are managed with a strong focus on information security.

Similarly, project management methodologies such as PRINCE2 or PMBOK can be used to support the design and transition of new or changed services, as required by ISO/IEC 20000-1.

In conclusion, while ISO/IEC 20000-1 provides a comprehensive standard for IT service management, it can be effectively used in conjunction with other frameworks and standards to provide a holistic approach to IT governance and management. The key to success is understanding the strengths of each approach and integrating them effectively to meet the specific needs of the organization.

Chapter 3: Service Management System (SMS)

The central engine that drives effective IT service management within an organization is the Service Management System (SMS). An SMS is more than a set of processes or a collection of tools; it is a holistic management system that provides a systematic approach to the delivery and improvement of IT services. The SMS not only incorporates service management policies, objectives, and processes, but it also includes the people, capabilities, resources, and supportive technology that enable its operation.

In this chapter, we will dive deep into the construct of a Service Management System as defined by ISO/IEC 20000-1. We'll explore how to design and implement an effective SMS that not only adheres to the standard but also brings tangible benefits to your organization. By providing clear guidelines on defining policies, objectives, and processes, this chapter will guide you through the vital steps needed to develop a robust SMS.

We will also explore the critical roles and responsibilities within the SMS, shedding light on how each role contributes to the overall efficiency and effectiveness of service management. Furthermore, we'll discuss the importance of continual improvement and performance monitoring, two components that ensure your SMS remains effective and continues to drive value for the business.

Chapter 3 is designed to help you understand the fundamental elements of an SMS, guide you in designing and implementing your own, and provide you with the necessary knowledge to continually improve and adapt it to your organization's evolving needs. Armed with this knowledge, you'll be equipped to build an SMS that not only complies with ISO/IEC 20000-1 but also brings about real-world improvements to the quality, consistency, and efficiency of your IT services.

3.1 Designing and Implementing an Effective SMS

The Service Management System (SMS) is the backbone of an organization's IT service management (ITSM) efforts. Designing and implementing an effective SMS is crucial to align IT services with business objectives, meet customer requirements, and facilitate continual improvement. The following sections outline a systematic approach to designing and implementing an SMS in line with the requirements of ISO/IEC 20000-1.

Defining the Scope of the SMS

The first step in designing an SMS is to define its scope clearly. This involves identifying the services, processes, locations, and parties involved that the SMS will cover. The scope should align with the strategic objectives of the organization and consider customer requirements, regulatory requirements, and the resources available.

Establishing the SMS Policy

An SMS policy provides a framework for the operation and governance of the SMS. It should reflect the organization's commitment to delivering quality IT services and continually improving SMS. The policy should be approved by top management and communicated to all personnel involved in the SMS. It should also be reviewed at regular intervals and updated as necessary.

Planning the SMS

The planning phase involves identifying the risks and opportunities associated with the SMS, establishing SMS objectives, and planning actions to address the risks and opportunities and achieve the SMS objectives. Risk management is crucial in planning the SMS and should consider both internal and external issues that can impact the SMS.

Implementing the SMS

The implementation of the SMS involves developing the necessary processes and procedures, providing resources, and assigning roles and responsibilities. A crucial element of implementing the SMS is ensuring that all personnel understand their roles and responsibilities and are competent to carry them out. Training may be required to ensure that personnel have the necessary skills and knowledge.

Documentation

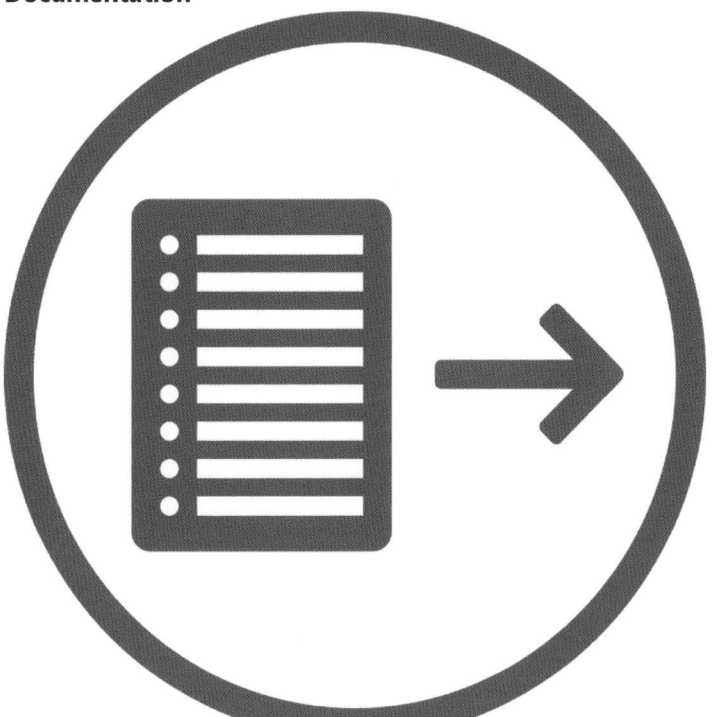

Proper documentation is a key aspect of the SMS. This includes not only the SMS policy and plans but also procedures, process maps, service level agreements, and records such as audit reports and management review records. Documentation should be controlled to ensure that it is accurate, up-to-date, and accessible to those who need it.

Performance Evaluation
Regular performance evaluation is crucial to ensure that the SMS is working effectively and delivering value. This involves monitoring, measurement, analysis, and evaluation of the SMS performance against the SMS objectives and service requirements. Internal audits and management reviews should be carried out at planned intervals to provide objective insight into the performance of the SMS.

Continual Improvement
One of the fundamental principles of ISO/IEC 20000-1 is the concept of continual improvement. The organization should proactively seek to improve the effectiveness and efficiency of the SMS and the services it delivers. This can be achieved through regular performance evaluation, identifying areas for improvement, and implementing improvement actions.

In conclusion, designing and implementing an effective SMS is not a one-off project but an ongoing process of planning, implementing, checking, and improving. It requires commitment and support from top management, clear communication, and involvement of all personnel. The benefits of an effective SMS, however, make it well worth the effort. An SMS that complies with ISO/IEC 20000-1 not only provides a framework for delivering quality IT services but also drives continual improvement, leading to enhanced customer satisfaction and business success.

3.2 Defining Policies, Objectives, and Processes

The Service Management System (SMS) sits at the core of any organization's ability to deliver effective IT services. To build an efficient SMS, one needs to articulate clear policies, define measurable objectives, and establish well-thought-out processes. Each of these elements plays a crucial role in shaping the overall operation of the SMS, contributing to the organization's ability to deliver services that meet business and customer requirements.

Defining Policies

Policies provide the guiding principles that underpin the SMS. They provide a direction for the organization's service management activities and serve as a reference point for decision-making. Policies should be clear, concise, and aligned with the organization's overall strategy and objectives.

For instance, the SMS policy should express the organization's commitment to service quality, customer satisfaction, and continual improvement. It should also provide a framework for setting and reviewing service management objectives. This policy should be endorsed by top management, communicated to all parties involved in service management, and reviewed regularly to ensure its ongoing suitability and effectiveness.

Additional policies may be required to govern specific aspects of service management, such as information security, risk management, change management, and incident management. These policies should align with the overarching SMS policy and provide clear guidance on the organization's approach to these areas.

Defining Objectives

Once policies are in place, the organization should define objectives that provide measurable targets for the SMS. These objectives should be Specific, Measurable, Achievable, Relevant, and Time-bound (SMART) and should align with the organization's service management policies and strategic goals.

Objectives might include targets for service availability, incident resolution times, customer satisfaction scores, or the successful implementation of changes. These objectives provide a way to measure the success of the SMS and should be monitored and reviewed regularly to drive continual improvement.

Establishing Processes

Processes are the operational aspect of the SMS. They define the sequence of activities that transform inputs into outputs, delivering services that meet customer and business requirements. Processes should be designed based on the objectives and policies, and they should be clearly documented, with defined inputs, outputs, controls, and activities.

Establishing effective processes involves identifying the required processes, defining their scope, objectives, and importance, and documenting their procedures. Key processes in the SMS might include service portfolio management, service level management, incident and problem management, change management, and continual improvement.

Each process should have a designated process owner who is responsible for ensuring that the process is fit for purpose and performing effectively. Additionally, the processes should be reviewed regularly for their efficiency and effectiveness, and improvements should be implemented based on these reviews.

By defining clear policies, objectives, and processes, organizations can establish a strong foundation for their SMS. These elements provide the direction, targets, and operational mechanisms that the SMS needs to deliver high-quality services and drive continual improvement. This, in turn, enables the organization to meet customer requirements, improve customer satisfaction, and align IT services with business objectives.

3.3 Roles and Responsibilities in the SMS

The effectiveness of a Service Management System (SMS) hinges on clearly defining and assigning roles and responsibilities. By doing so, organizations ensure that everyone understands their part in the system, fostering accountability and enabling efficient, effective service delivery. This section will discuss the key roles within an SMS and their associated responsibilities based on the ISO/IEC 20000-1 standard.

Top Management

In the context of an SMS, top management refers to individuals or groups at the highest levels of the organization who have the authority to coordinate the strategic direction of IT services. Their responsibilities include:

- Establishing the service management policy and ensuring it aligns with the organization's strategic direction.

- Ensuring that service management objectives are established and are compatible with the strategic direction.

- Providing the necessary resources for the establishment, implementation, maintenance, and continual improvement of the SMS.

- Communicating the importance of effective service management and conforming to SMS requirements.

Service Management System Manager

The Service Management System Manager has the day-to-day responsibility for coordinating the operation of the SMS. Their responsibilities include:

- Overseeing the design and implementation of service management processes and procedures.

- Ensuring compliance with the service management policy and objectives.

- Reporting on the performance of the SMS to top management.

- Identifying opportunities for improvement and driving the implementation of improvement actions.

Process Owners

Each service management process should have a designated Process Owner. The Process Owner is responsible for:

- Ensuring the process is designed to meet the agreed objectives.
- Overseeing the operation of the process and ensuring it delivers the desired outcomes.
- Coordinating with other Process Owners to ensure that the processes work together effectively.
- Identifying and implementing opportunities for process improvement.

Service Owners

The Service Owner is accountable for a specific service within the service portfolio. Their responsibilities include:

- Acting as a primary point of contact for all issues related to their service.
- Working with Process Owners to ensure that the service is delivered effectively.
- Ensuring that the service meets the agreed service level targets and customer requirements.
- Driving improvement in the delivery of their service.

Other Roles

Depending on the size and nature of the organization, there may be other roles involved in service management, such as Service Desk Staff, Incident Managers, Change Managers, and IT Operations Staff. Each of these roles will have specific responsibilities relating to their area of work, and these should be clearly defined and communicated.

In conclusion, clearly defined roles and responsibilities are crucial to the effectiveness of an SMS. They ensure that everyone involved in service management knows what they are supposed to do and how their work contributes to the delivery of high-quality IT services. A clear understanding of roles and responsibilities also supports accountability and fosters a culture of continual improvement, both of which are essential for successful service management.

3.4 Continual Improvement and Performance Monitoring

Continual improvement and performance monitoring are two foundational aspects of a well-functioning Service Management System (SMS). They ensure that the SMS not only delivers on its current goals but also evolves over time to better meet the organization's changing needs and objectives. The following sections detail how to implement and maintain these aspects within the SMS, as outlined in ISO/IEC 20000-1.

Continual Improvement

Continual improvement is a cyclical process of identifying opportunities for improvement, implementing actions to realize these improvements, evaluating the effectiveness of these actions, and then identifying further opportunities based on these evaluations. The ultimate goal is to enhance the organization's service management capabilities and the quality of the IT services it provides.

Continual improvement in an SMS should be strategic and systematic. This involves establishing an improvement framework, which includes defining improvement objectives aligned with the organization's strategic goals, developing a plan to achieve these objectives, implementing the plan, and then reviewing and adjusting the plan based on the results.

The 'Plan-Do-Check-Act' (PDCA) cycle is a popular method for managing continual improvement. This involves:

i. Plan: Identify improvement opportunities, define objectives, and plan actions.

ii. Do: Implement the improvement actions.

iii. Check: Monitor and measure the results against the objectives.

iv. Act: Review the results and adjust the plan as necessary.

Performance Monitoring

Performance monitoring is the ongoing process of gathering and analyzing data to evaluate how well the SMS is performing. This provides a basis for decision-making, enables the organization to identify potential issues before they become problems, and drives continual improvement.

Performance monitoring in an SMS should focus on both process performance and service performance:

- **Process Performance:** This involves monitoring how well the service management processes are working. Key metrics might include the efficiency of processes (how quickly and cost-effectively they deliver their outputs) and their effectiveness (how well the outputs meet the desired outcomes).

- **Service Performance:** This involves monitoring the quality of the IT services being provided. Key metrics might include service availability, reliability, and responsiveness, as well as customer satisfaction.

Performance monitoring requires the establishment of Key Performance Indicators (KPIs) that align with the organization's service management objectives. These KPIs should be measurable, actionable, relevant, and time-bound (SMART) and should provide a balanced view of performance.

In summary, continual improvement and performance monitoring are key to maintaining an effective SMS. They enable the organization to assess the current performance of the SMS, identify areas for improvement, and make informed decisions about how to improve. This not only helps to enhance the quality of IT services and customer satisfaction but also enables the organization to better align its IT services with its strategic objectives. By embracing continual improvement and performance monitoring, organizations can ensure that their SMS remains effective and valuable in a changing business environment.

Chapter 4: Planning and Implementing Service Management Processes

Successful Service Management Systems (SMS) are underpinned by well-defined and effectively executed service management processes. This chapter delves into the crucial aspects of planning and implementing these processes, as guided by ISO/IEC 20000-1. From formulating service strategies and designing services to managing incidents and changes, every stage in the lifecycle of IT services involves intricate processes that require careful planning and management.

We will explore the critical phases of service strategy, design, transition, and operation, with a focus on the key processes within each of these stages. The aim is to provide a comprehensive understanding of how these processes come together to facilitate the delivery of high-quality IT services that meet business and customer requirements.

In addition, the chapter will also shed light on some of the more specialized processes, such as service level management, service reporting, service continuity and availability management, and supplier and relationship management. Each of these processes plays a unique role within the broader service management context and is vital to the overall effectiveness of an SMS.

By the end of this chapter, you should have a deeper understanding of how to plan, implement, and manage the various service management processes within your organization. This knowledge will equip you to construct a robust and effective SMS, align your IT services with your business goals, and consistently deliver value to your customers.

4.1 Service Strategy and Design Processes

Service Strategy and Design are two crucial stages in the lifecycle of IT services, setting the direction and the detailed specifications for services that will meet business needs and provide value to customers. Understanding these processes in line with the ISO/IEC 20000-1 standard is critical to the successful implementation of a Service Management System (SMS).

Service Strategy

Service Strategy is about ensuring that the organization's IT services are aligned with its business objectives and are capable of delivering the required value. This involves understanding the current and future needs of the business, as well as the needs of its customers, and developing a strategic approach to meet these needs.

Key processes within Service Strategy include:

- **Strategy Management for IT Services**: This involves defining the direction and goals for IT services based on an understanding of the organization's business strategy, current capabilities, and market conditions. This includes identifying opportunities for new services, as well as ways to improve existing services.

- **Financial Management for IT Services**: This involves managing the financial aspects of IT services, including budgeting, costing, and charging. This helps to ensure that the organization can afford to provide the IT services it needs, that customers understand what they are paying for, and that the organization is getting value for its IT investments.

- **Demand Management**: This involves understanding and managing the demand for IT services. This includes predicting future demand, managing current demand, and shaping demand to align with the organization's capabilities and objectives.

Service Design

Once the Service Strategy has been defined, the next stage is Service Design. This involves turning the strategic objectives into detailed specifications for IT services. This includes designing the service solutions, the service portfolio, and the service management processes needed to deliver and support the services.

Key processes within Service Design include:

- **Design Coordination**: This involves coordinating all design activities, resources, and processes. This ensures that the various elements of the service design are integrated and aligned with the organization's business objectives.

- **Service Catalogue Management**: This involves managing the service catalog, which is a database or document that contains information about all live IT services. The service catalog is an essential tool for communicating about IT services, managing demand, and delivering value.

- **Service Level Management**: This involves negotiating, agreeing on, and documenting Service Level Agreements (SLAs) with customers, as well as ensuring that these SLAs are met. SLAs define the level of service that the customer can expect, and Service Level Management is critical for managing expectations and delivering customer satisfaction.

- **Capacity Management**: This involves ensuring that the organization has sufficient capacity to meet the current and future demand for IT services. This includes managing the performance of IT services, as well as planning for future capacity needs.

- **Availability Management**: This involves ensuring that IT services are available when needed. This includes managing the reliability and recoverability of IT services.

- **IT Service Continuity Management**: This involves ensuring that the organization can continue to deliver critical IT services during a disaster or major incident. This includes planning, testing, and implementing disaster recovery plans.

In conclusion, Service Strategy and Design are two critical stages in the service management lifecycle. They set the direction for IT services and turn this direction into detailed plans and specifications. By understanding and effectively managing these processes, organizations can ensure that their IT services are aligned with their business needs, are capable of delivering value, and are designed to deliver high-quality, reliable service.

4.2 Service Transition and Service Operation Processes

Once the service strategy has been established and the service design detailed, the next steps in the service lifecycle, as per ISO/IEC 20000-1, are Service Transition and Service Operation. Both stages play pivotal roles in bringing the service from its conceptual stage to full operation and then ensuring it delivers value to the customers on an ongoing basis.

Service Transition

Service Transition is the stage where the service design is realized and the service is prepared for deployment into the live environment. It involves the careful planning and coordination of resources and processes to ensure that the transition is smooth, the risk is managed, and the service will deliver the expected outcomes. The main goal of this phase is to ensure that changes to services and service management processes are carried out in a coordinated way.

Key processes within Service Transition include:

- **Change Management**: This involves managing all changes to the IT infrastructure, including software, hardware, processes, and documentation. The aim is to handle changes in a controlled manner, minimizing the risk of disruptions to services and ensuring that changes deliver the expected benefits.

- **Service Asset and Configuration Management**: This process is concerned with maintaining information about the configuration of services and the assets that support them. This configuration information is used to manage and control the assets and to support many other service management processes.

- **Release and Deployment Management**: This process is responsible for the planning, scheduling, and controlling of the movement of releases to test and live environments. The aim is to ensure that all releases are tested, verified, and deployed efficiently and that the integrity of the live environment is protected.

- **Knowledge Management**: This involves gathering, organizing, and making available knowledge that can help the organization improve its services and processes. This can involve creating a knowledge base, organizing information in a way that it can be easily accessed and used, and encouraging sharing and use of knowledge across the organization.

Service Operation

Service Operation is the phase where the services are in live operation, delivering value to the customers. This stage involves managing the day-to-day operation of the services, dealing with incidents and requests, and ensuring that the services meet the agreed-upon service levels.

Key processes within Service Operation include:

- **Event Management**: This involves monitoring all events that occur in the IT infrastructure to detect any deviations from the norm that could impact services. The goal is to identify and respond to events in a way that minimizes any negative impact on the business.

- **Incident Management**: This process is responsible for managing the lifecycle of all incidents. The primary objective is to restore normal service operations as quickly as possible and minimize the adverse impact on business operations.

- **Problem Management**: This process manages the lifecycle of all problems. Its primary objectives are to prevent incidents from happening and to minimize the impact of incidents that cannot be prevented. It focuses on identifying and managing the root causes of incidents.

- **Request Fulfillment**: This process is responsible for managing the lifecycle of all service requests from users. It provides a channel for users to request and receive standard services and also assists with general information, complaints, and comments.

- **Access Management**: This process is responsible for allowing users to make use of a service or group of services. It ensures authorized users have the right to use a service while preventing access to non-authorized users.

In summary, Service Transition and Service Operation are essential stages in the lifecycle of IT services. They turn the service design into a working, live service and then manage the operation of this service to deliver value to customers. By understanding and effectively managing these processes, organizations can ensure a smooth transition of services into operation and maintain a high quality of service that meets the needs of their customers.

4.3 Incident Management and Problem Management

In the realm of IT Service Management (ITSM), incident and problem management are crucial processes designed to restore normal service operation as quickly as possible after a disruption and to minimize the adverse impact on business operations. Understanding these two concepts, their similarities, differences, and interrelation, is vital for any organization aiming to improve their service delivery in line with ISO/IEC 20000-1.

Incident Management

Incident Management is the process responsible for managing the lifecycle of all incidents. An incident is defined as an unplanned interruption to an IT service or a reduction in the quality of an IT service. The primary objective of incident management is to restore normal service operations as quickly as possible to minimize the adverse impact on business operations.

Incident management begins with incident identification, where issues are logged, categorized based on their type and severity, and recorded in an incident management system. The incidents could be reported by users, identified by an IT staff member, or automatically detected and logged by system monitoring tools.

Following identification, the incident moves into the investigation and diagnosis phase. This involves understanding the nature of the incident, what caused it, and how it can be resolved. Throughout this phase, communication with the affected users is crucial to manage their expectations and keep them informed about the progress of resolution efforts.

After a solution or workaround has been identified, the incident is resolved and closed. However, the resolution is not merely about fixing the problem; it's also about ensuring the user is satisfied with the solution and the service they've received. Post-incident review or analysis is often carried out to understand how the incident occurred, how it was handled, and how similar incidents can be prevented in the future.

Problem Management

Problem Management, on the other hand, focuses on identifying and managing the root causes of incidents and finding ways to prevent future incidents. A problem is a cause, or potential cause, of one or more incidents. The primary objectives of problem management are to prevent incidents from happening and to minimize the impact of incidents that cannot be prevented.

Problem Management includes two sub-processes: Reactive Problem Management, which is generally triggered as a response to an incident(s), and Proactive Problem Management, aimed at identifying and solving problems and known errors before incidents occur in relation to these.

Proactive Problem Management makes use of data and information from other service management processes to identify trends or points of weakness. It involves activities like trend analysis, target setting for improvement, providing information to enable other service management processes to prevent recurrence, and arranging training and awareness sessions.

The goal of problem management is not just to resolve the problems that cause incidents but to manage these problems in a way that leads to reduced incident volumes, better-managed incidents, and, ultimately, improved service quality.

The Interrelation of Incident and Problem Management

While incident management focuses on resolving incidents quickly and efficiently, problem management goes a step further to identify and deal with the root causes of these incidents. These two processes, while distinct, should ideally be closely aligned.

The incident management process may trigger the problem management process when incidents are recurring or when an incident is so severe that it's critical to identify and address the root cause to prevent a recurrence. Conversely, the problem management process may use information from the incident management process to identify trends or patterns that might suggest an underlying problem.

In conclusion, both incident and problem management are crucial elements in maintaining high-quality IT service as guided by ISO/IEC 20000-1. An effective ITSM approach will integrate these processes, using incident management to maintain service quality in the short term and problem management to improve it in the long term. Through understanding and properly applying both, organizations can significantly improve their ability to deliver reliable, high-quality IT services that support their business objectives.

4.4 Change Management and Configuration Management

Change Management and Configuration Management are two essential elements within the IT Service Management (ITSM) lifecycle. Both play critical roles in maintaining the stability and reliability of services while allowing for necessary modifications and improvements. Understanding these processes and their application as guided by the ISO/IEC 20000-1 standard is crucial for effective ITSM implementation.

Change Management

Change Management is a structured approach to transitioning individuals, teams, and organizations from a current state to a desired future state. In the context of ITSM, it is a formal process used for controlling the lifecycle of all changes, enabling beneficial changes to be made with minimum disruption to IT services.

Changes are often necessary to enhance service quality, respond to evolving business needs, address issues or risks, or accommodate new technological advancements. However, uncontrolled or poorly managed changes can have negative impacts, such as service downtime or degraded service quality.

The change management process typically includes several key stages:

- **Request for Change (RFC)**: The process begins when a request for a change is made. This could be in response to a problem, an identified opportunity for improvement, a regulatory requirement, or a number of other triggers.

- **Change Assessment**: Once a request for change has been made, it's essential to assess the impact, costs, benefits, and risks associated with the change. This ensures that only beneficial changes are approved and helps in planning and managing the change.

- **Approve or Reject**: Based on the assessment, the change may be approved or rejected. Approved changes are then scheduled and communicated to all relevant stakeholders.

- **Implement the Change**: Once approved, the change is implemented, carefully following a pre-defined plan.

- **Review and Close**: After a change has been implemented, it's necessary to review the change to ensure it has achieved its intended outcomes and hasn't resulted in any unexpected issues. If the change is successful, it can be formally closed.

Configuration Management

Configuration Management, on the other hand, focuses on establishing and maintaining consistency of a product's performance and its functional and physical attributes with its requirements, design, and operational information throughout its life. In ITSM, Configuration Management is concerned with the management of all configuration items (CIs) within an IT infrastructure.

A Configuration Item could be any component of an IT system that needs to be managed in order to deliver an IT service and can include hardware, software, buildings, people, and formal documentation such as process documentation and service level agreements.

The key activities of Configuration Management include:

- **Configuration Identification**: This involves specifying and identifying the CIs within the system and documenting their functional and physical characteristics in a configuration identification document.

- **Configuration Control**: This activity involves managing changes, either through an approval process or through a set of documented procedures, to prevent unauthorized changes to CIs.

- **Configuration Status Accounting**: This activity involves recording and reporting all the necessary information on the status of the development process.

- **Configuration Auditing**: This activity verifies that the configurations of a system perform as expected and are consistent with the specified requirements.

- **Configuration Documentation**: The entire configuration management process must be documented in a configuration management plan.

Interrelation of Change and Configuration Management

Change Management and Configuration Management are closely related and often interact with each other. A proposed change will often involve one or more CIs, and the Configuration Management system provides the information necessary to assess the impact of the change.

On the other hand, any approved change should be reflected in the Configuration Management System (CMS). This means that when changes are made, the CMS should be updated to reflect the new configuration of the affected CI or CIs.

In conclusion, both Change Management and Configuration Management play critical roles in the ITSM lifecycle. Understanding their key processes and how they interact can help organizations to manage their IT services more effectively, increase stability and control, and ultimately deliver higher service quality as per ISO/IEC 20000-1 guidelines.

4.5 Release and Deployment Management

Release and Deployment Management is a crucial process within the scope of IT Service Management (ITSM). This process aims to ensure the integrity of a live environment is protected and that the correct components are released. The ISO/IEC 20000-1 standard offers guidelines on how to manage the release and deployment processes effectively, thus enabling organizations to improve service quality and efficiency.

Release Management

Release Management is the process of managing, planning, scheduling, and controlling a build through different stages and environments, including testing and deploying software releases. A 'release' refers to a collection of hardware, software, configuration items, and other components that are required to implement one or more approved changes to IT services.

The primary objective of release management is to ensure that only tested and verified releases are moved into production and that they contribute the maximum possible benefit to the organization while minimizing the impact of incidents upon service.

The release management process usually includes the following steps:

- **Release Planning**: This step involves defining the scope of the release, building a release schedule, and identifying the resources required.

- **Design and Build**: In this step, the release package is designed and built based on the requirements defined in the release plan.

- **Testing**: The release package is then tested to ensure that it meets the defined requirements and does not introduce any additional issues.

- **Deployment**: Once the release package has been tested and approved, it is deployed into the production environment.

- **Review and Close**: Following deployment, the release is reviewed to ensure that it has achieved its objectives and that any lessons learned are documented for future releases.

Deployment Management

Deployment Management, on the other hand, is a process of moving components, such as configuration items, from one environment to another. In ITSM, deployment management is concerned with transferring new or changed software, hardware, processes, or documentation from the development environment to the live environment.

Deployment management involves several key stages:

- **Release Preparation**: This includes preparing the release package and the environment where it will be deployed.

- **Deployment**: This is the stage where the release is actually transferred to the live environment. The deployment should be carried out in a controlled manner, with a rollback plan in place in case any issues occur.

- **Post-deployment Testing**: After the release has been deployed, it should be tested to confirm that it works as expected in the live environment.

- **Performance Monitoring**: Once the release is live, it should be continuously monitored to ensure that it performs as expected and to detect any issues as early as possible.

- **Review and Close**: Finally, the deployment is reviewed, and any lessons learned are documented for future deployments.

The Interrelation of Release and Deployment Management

While Release and Deployment Management are distinct processes, they are closely related and often overlap. Release Management focuses on the planning, design, build, configuration, and testing of software and hardware to create a 'release' that can deliver a new service or update an existing one. Deployment Management is the next step, focusing on the transition of this 'release' from the development environment to the live environment.

Together, Release and Deployment Management play a crucial role in minimizing risks associated with the introduction of new services or changes to existing ones, ensuring that they are introduced in a controlled manner and deliver the expected benefits. By following the guidelines set out in the ISO/IEC 20000-1 standard, organizations can use these processes to improve the quality of their IT services and deliver more value to their customers.

4.6 Service Level Management and Service Reporting

Service Level Management and Service Reporting are key processes in the IT Service Management (ITSM) framework that help organizations meet business expectations, monitor service performance, and communicate effectively with stakeholders. Both are integral parts of the ISO/IEC 20000-1 standard, contributing to a successful and efficient service management system.

Service Level Management

Service Level Management is the process of defining, managing, and monitoring the levels of IT services specified in Service Level Agreements (SLAs). The primary objective of Service Level Management is to ensure that all current and planned IT services are delivered to agreed achievable targets. This process involves constant liaison with the business to negotiate and agree on service levels.

Service Level Management generally includes the following steps:

- **Identify Service Requirements**: Firstly, it is important to identify the services that the organization provides and to understand their associated requirements. This involves talking to stakeholders to understand their needs and expectations.

- **Develop and Negotiate SLAs**: Once the service requirements are understood, the next step is to develop SLAs. These are agreements between the IT service provider and the customer that outline the expected level of service. SLAs are typically negotiated and agreed upon by both parties.

- **Monitor Service Performance**: After SLAs are in place, it is important to monitor the actual performance of services against the agreed-upon levels. This often involves collecting and analyzing data related to service performance.

- **Review and Improve Services**: The last step in the process is to review the performance of services regularly and identify opportunities for improvement. This can involve renegotiating SLAs, improving service delivery, or making changes to the IT infrastructure.

Service Reporting

Service Reporting, on the other hand, is the process of producing and distributing reports that provide information about the performance of IT services. This enables informed decisions to be made based on the performance and capacity of IT services and infrastructure and supports effective communication with stakeholders.

A good service report will typically include information such as:

- **Performance Metrics**: This could include measures of service availability, reliability, and responsiveness.

- **SLA Compliance**: It is important to report on whether services are meeting the levels defined in their SLAs.

- **Incidents and Problems**: The report should provide information about any incidents or problems that have occurred and how they were resolved.

- **Customer Feedback**: If available, customer feedback can provide valuable information about the perceived quality of IT services.

Interrelation of Service Level Management and Service Reporting

Service Level Management and Service Reporting are closely related processes. Service Reporting is a vital part of Service Level Management, as it provides the data needed to monitor and review service performance. Regular service reports allow IT managers to assess whether services are meeting their SLAs and to identify any trends or issues that may need to be addressed.

On the other hand, Service Level Management informs Service Reporting by defining what should be measured and reported. The targets set in SLAs will often form the basis for performance metrics that are included in service reports.

In conclusion, Service Level Management and Service Reporting are crucial to the successful delivery of IT services. They help to ensure that services meet business needs and provide a mechanism for continual monitoring and improvement. Following the guidelines set out in the ISO/IEC 20000-1 standard can help organizations to implement these processes effectively and to deliver high-quality IT services.

4.7 Service Continuity and Availability Management

Service Continuity and Availability Management are critical elements of IT Service Management (ITSM) that ensure the constant availability of services, even during adverse events, and that the organization is prepared to recover and continue its operations effectively. The ISO/IEC 20000-1 standard emphasizes the importance of these processes for maintaining service quality and satisfying customer needs.

Service Continuity Management

Service Continuity Management (SCM) is a process that focuses on how to restore and recover critical services and operations after a disruption or disaster. It involves identifying essential services, assessing risks, creating contingency plans, and ensuring that an organization can recover within a predefined timeframe.

The primary steps in Service Continuity Management are:

- **Business Impact Analysis (BIA)**: BIA is a method for identifying the services and processes that are critical for the business and understanding the impact of their unavailability over time.

- **Risk Assessment**: This involves identifying and evaluating the risks that can cause the disruption of critical services. It includes analyzing both the likelihood and the impact of potential risks.

- **Develop Continuity Plans**: Based on the findings from the BIA and Risk Assessment, continuity plans are developed. These plans detail the actions, resources, and procedures necessary to restore services in the event of a disruption.

- **Testing and Exercising**: Continuity plans should be regularly tested and exercised to ensure they are effective and that staff are familiar with them.

- **Continuous Improvement**: After testing, plans should be reviewed and updated regularly to ensure that they remain relevant as the business and its environment evolve.

Availability Management

Availability Management (AM) focuses on ensuring that IT services and infrastructure are available to meet agreed-upon service level targets. It involves proactive measures to improve the reliability, maintainability, and serviceability of IT services and components.

Key activities in Availability Management include:

- **Availability Requirements**: Understand and document the availability requirements of the business. This may involve negotiating service level agreements (SLAs) that specify availability targets.

- **Design for Availability**: Availability should be considered from the earliest stages of service design. This includes selecting technologies and architectures that are resilient and can support the required levels of availability.

- **Monitoring and Reporting**: Availability should be continuously monitored, and reports should be produced to inform stakeholders of performance against targets.

- **Reliability, Maintainability, and Serviceability Improvements**: Analyzing the causes of unavailability and identifying improvements in reliability, maintainability, and serviceability.

Interrelation of Service Continuity and Availability Management

Service Continuity and Availability Management, while distinct, are closely related and complementary processes:

- Availability Management is proactive, focusing on ensuring that services are available during normal operations, while Service Continuity Management is reactive, focusing on restoring services after a major incident.

- Service Continuity Management can be viewed as a subset of Availability Management for situations where availability is critically impacted.

- The risk assessment aspect of Service Continuity can inform Availability Management by identifying potential points of failure that need to be addressed proactively.

- Availability Management contributes to Service Continuity by ensuring that there are fewer disruptions, to begin with and by ensuring that systems are designed in such a way as to minimize recovery time when disruptions do occur.

In conclusion, Service Continuity and Availability Management are essential for any organization that relies on IT services to support its business operations. By effectively managing these processes in line with the ISO/IEC 20000-1 standard, organizations can reduce the impact of service disruptions, improve customer satisfaction, and safeguard their reputation and bottom line. Implementing both processes provides a comprehensive approach to ensuring that critical services are available when needed and that the organization is prepared to respond effectively to any disruptions.

4.8 Supplier Management and Relationship Management

In the world of IT Service Management (ITSM), Supplier Management and Relationship Management are pivotal processes that ensure the smooth functioning and delivery of services. They play a significant role in the ISO/IEC 20000-1 standard, fostering an efficient service management system that integrates well with external parties and stakeholders.

Supplier Management

Supplier Management involves identifying, selecting, contracting, managing, and reviewing suppliers to ensure that they are able to meet the organization's requirements for IT services. Supplier

Management ensures that the organization's operations are not disrupted due to issues related to suppliers and that the best value is obtained from them.

Key activities in Supplier Management include:

- **Supplier Evaluation and Selection**: This process includes identifying potential suppliers, evaluating their ability to meet requirements, and selecting those that offer the best value.

- **Contract Negotiation and Management**: After selecting suppliers, contracts must be negotiated, agreed upon, and managed. This includes defining and agreeing on service levels, costs, and responsibilities.

- **Performance Monitoring**: It's critical to continually monitor suppliers' performance against the agreed contract terms, including delivery timelines, service levels, and costs. Regular reviews and audits should be carried out to ensure compliance.

- **Relationship Management with Suppliers**: Establishing and maintaining good relationships with suppliers can help to ensure smooth service delivery and better response to issues when they arise.

- **Supplier Risk Management**: Identifying and managing risks related to suppliers, such as the risk of supply failure or issues with quality, is an essential part of Supplier Management.

Relationship Management

In the context of ITSM, Relationship Management refers to establishing and nurturing the relationships between the IT service provider and its customers, users, and other stakeholders. It involves understanding the needs and expectations of these stakeholders and ensuring that the IT service provider can meet these needs.

Key activities in Relationship Management include:

- **Stakeholder Identification**: Identify who the stakeholders are, what their interests and influence are, and how they interact with the IT services.

- **Relationship Building**: Develop relationships with stakeholders based on understanding their needs, expectations, and the value they require from the IT services.

- **Communication**: Maintain open and effective communication channels with all stakeholders. This includes keeping them informed of changes, issues, and improvements, as well as understanding and managing their perceptions and satisfaction.

- **Stakeholder Engagement**: Engage stakeholders in decisions and changes that affect them. This can help to ensure buy-in and support for IT services.

Interrelation of Supplier Management and Relationship Management

While Supplier Management and Relationship Management are distinct processes, they are closely related and often intersect:

- Suppliers can be considered key stakeholders in an IT service provider's ecosystem, and therefore, effective Relationship Management techniques can be applied to manage relationships with suppliers.

- Both processes involve understanding and managing the expectations of external parties (whether they are customers, users, or suppliers) and ensuring that these expectations are met.

- Effective Supplier Management can enhance Relationship Management by ensuring that services are delivered effectively and efficiently, which can increase customer and user satisfaction.

In conclusion, both Supplier Management and Relationship Management are crucial to the successful delivery of IT services. By understanding and managing the needs and expectations of suppliers, customers, users, and other stakeholders, an organization can ensure that its IT services are effective, efficient, and aligned with business objectives. Adherence to the principles and practices of these processes, as outlined in the ISO/IEC 20000-1 standard, can enhance an organization's service delivery and contribute to its overall success.

Chapter 5: Service Measurement and Reporting

In the constantly evolving landscape of IT Service Management (ITSM), a systematic approach to service measurement and reporting is integral to maintaining high service quality and achieving continual service improvement. As the saying goes, "you can't manage what you can't measure."

Chapter 5 of this book, "Service Measurement and Reporting," delves into the importance of these activities in the context of the ISO/IEC 20000-1 standard. It lays the groundwork for understanding how to define key performance indicators (KPIs), the process of data collection, analysis, and reporting, the importance of effective communication in service reporting, and how benchmarking and best practices contribute to an organization's growth and maturity.

At its core, Service Measurement and Reporting provides the necessary visibility into the performance of IT services. It serves as the eyes and ears of the service provider, helping to identify gaps, measure progress, and evaluate the success of initiatives and improvements. This chapter will guide you through the best practices for setting up a comprehensive measurement and reporting system that not only aligns with ISO/IEC 20000-1 but also contributes to the overall effectiveness of your service management efforts.

Whether you're an ITSM professional, a manager responsible for service delivery, or a senior executive aiming to steer your organization toward service excellence, this chapter will equip you with the knowledge and insights needed to effectively measure and report on your service performance. With the right tools, techniques, and understanding, you can turn data into actionable insights, providing the information necessary to make informed decisions, prioritize initiatives, and deliver consistent value to your customers and business stakeholders.

5.1 Defining Key Performance Indicators (KPIs)

Key Performance Indicators (KPIs) are essential for any IT Service Management (ITSM) strategy as they allow organizations to measure the effectiveness and efficiency of their IT services. KPIs, when designed well and used effectively, provide a quantifiable measurement of performance, helping to drive improvements, validate achievements, and indicate when corrective actions are necessary. The process of defining KPIs must be a thoughtful exercise, aligning closely with organizational goals and objectives and tailored to the specifics of individual services and processes.

In the context of the ISO/IEC 20000-1 standard, KPIs are instrumental in enabling organizations to measure and monitor their compliance with the standard's requirements and thereby drive continual service improvement.

The Role of KPIs in ITSM

KPIs play a crucial role in ITSM by providing clear, measurable values that gauge the performance of IT services and processes against defined objectives. They help organizations to:

- Understand how well they are performing in relation to their strategic goals.

- Identify areas for improvement and track the effectiveness of implemented changes.

- Make informed decisions based on data and trends rather than assumptions.

- Demonstrate the value of IT services to stakeholders and align IT objectives with business objectives.

Defining Effective KPIs

The process of defining KPIs should be systematic, starting with a clear understanding of the organization's goals and objectives. Here are some essential steps for defining effective KPIs:

- **Understand Business Goals**: Before defining KPIs, it is important to have a deep understanding of your organization's strategic goals and how your IT services contribute to these goals.

- **Identify Critical Success Factors (CSFs)**: CSFs are elements that are vital for a strategy to be successful. For IT services, this might include factors such as the availability and reliability of services, customer satisfaction levels, or the efficiency of service delivery processes.

- **Define KPIs Based on CSFs**: Once the CSFs are identified, you can define KPIs that will measure the performance against these factors. Each KPI should be tied directly to a CSF and ultimately to the strategic goals of the organization.

- **Ensure KPIs are SMART**: KPIs should be Specific, Measurable, Achievable, Relevant, and Time-bound. This means that they should clearly define what is to be measured, how it will be measured, what the target value is, why it is important, and the timeframe for measurement.

- **Establish Baselines and Targets**: It's crucial to establish a baseline (the current state) for each KPI and define what the target state (desired level of performance) is. This provides a clear measure of improvement over time.

- **Review and Refine**: KPIs should not be static. They should be regularly reviewed and refined as necessary to ensure they continue to be relevant and useful in measuring performance.

Examples of KPIs in ITSM

While KPIs will vary between organizations and services, here are a few examples of common KPIs used in ITSM:

- **Incident Management**: Time to resolve incidents, the number of incidents resolved at first contact, and the percentage of incidents escalated.

- **Change Management**: Percentage of successful changes, number of emergency changes, and the number of changes rolled back.

- **Service Level Management**: Percentage of service targets met, number of service level breaches.

- **Problem Management**: Average time to resolve problems, the number of recurring incidents.

- **Availability Management**: Percentage of uptime, the number of service outages.

Defining KPIs is a critical part of setting up a successful service management system. By focusing on the right performance indicators, organizations can drive improvements in their IT services, deliver greater value to the business, and achieve compliance with standards like ISO/IEC 20000-1.

5.2 Data Collection, Analysis, and Reporting

In the context of IT Service Management (ITSM) and the ISO/IEC 20000-1 standard, the process of data collection, analysis, and reporting is crucial. It provides the organization with valuable insights into the performance of its services and processes, helps to identify areas for improvement, and ensures that service objectives align with the business objectives.

Data Collection

The first step in this process is data collection. This involves gathering information from a variety of sources to track the Key Performance Indicators (KPIs) defined for your IT services and processes.

Data collection might involve automatically capturing logs from service management tools, conducting surveys to gather feedback from users, recording details about incidents and problems, or manually tracking other metrics relevant to the performance of your services.

It's crucial that data is collected consistently, accurately, and in a way that's repeatable. This enables you to track trends over time and provides a reliable basis for making decisions. In order to facilitate efficient data collection, organizations may need to invest in automated tools, integrate systems, and establish clear processes for capturing and recording data.

Data Analysis

Once data has been collected, it needs to be analyzed to provide insights. Data analysis involves processing the collected data to identify patterns, trends, and anomalies. This could include calculating averages, identifying peaks and troughs, comparing performance against targets, or looking for correlations between different data points.

For example, an analysis might reveal that the average resolution time for incidents has been increasing over the past few months, suggesting a potential issue with your incident management process. Or, it might show a correlation between the introduction of a particular type of change and an increase in incidents, indicating a problem with your change management process.

Effective data analysis requires a combination of good tools, analytical skills, and a deep understanding of your IT services and the business context in which they operate. The aim is not just to crunch numbers but to provide meaningful insights that help the organization improve its service delivery.

Data Reporting

The final step in the process is data reporting. This involves communicating the results of your data analysis to stakeholders in a clear, concise, and meaningful way.

Reports should be tailored to the audience. For example, a technical team might need detailed reports on incident trends to help them identify and resolve issues, while senior management might need a high-level dashboard showing whether service level targets are being met.

Good reporting provides transparency about the performance of your IT services, demonstrates the value that IT is delivering to the business, and helps to inform decision-making. It's also a key requirement of the ISO/IEC 20000-1 standard, which expects organizations to measure and report on their service performance.

In the end, the cycle of data collection, analysis, and reporting should be a continuous process, constantly providing insights to drive improvements and align IT services with business needs. This forms the basis of a data-driven approach to ITSM, supporting the achievement of strategic goals and ensuring compliance with standards like ISO/IEC 20000-1.

5.3 Service Reporting and Communication

Service reporting and communication are two essential aspects of IT Service Management (ITSM). In accordance with the ISO/IEC 20000-1 standard, they both are critical to maintaining a healthy relationship between IT service providers and their stakeholders. Stakeholders could include internal personnel, customers, suppliers, and the wider organization. Effective reporting and communication can greatly influence service perception and satisfaction and form an integral part of continual service improvement.

Service Reporting

Service reporting is the process of creating and distributing periodic reports that contain detailed information about the performance of IT services. This performance is typically assessed against previously defined Key Performance Indicators (KPIs) and Service Level Agreements (SLAs).

Effective service reporting serves multiple purposes:

- **Performance Overview**: It provides an overview of the service's performance against set targets, offering insights into how well the service is doing.

- **Trend Analysis**: It helps identify trends over time, highlighting areas of consistent performance or signifying where improvement is needed.

- **Decision-Making**: It informs decision-making processes and aids in the planning and implementation of improvements.

- **Demonstrating Value**: It demonstrates the value that the IT service provider brings to the organization, supporting the perception of IT as a strategic partner rather than a cost center.

- **Transparency**: It brings transparency, allowing all stakeholders to understand the current status of the services.

Creating effective service reports requires a clear understanding of what the audience is interested in and the challenges they face. For example, senior management might be interested in high-level performance against business objectives, while operational staff might need detailed performance data to help identify issues and solutions.

Service Communication

Communication in ITSM is as vital as the services themselves. Good communication practices ensure that all stakeholders have the appropriate level of information about services, such as changes, incidents, and planned improvements.

Service communication should:

- Be clear, concise, and appropriate to the audience.
- Use the channels that best reach the target audience.
- Ensure two-way communication to capture and respond to feedback and questions.

There are various aspects to service communication:

- **Operational Communication**: This includes communication regarding incidents, problems, and changes. It should be timely and clear to minimize disruption to the service users.
- **Tactical Communication**: This includes communication regarding service performance and improvement plans. It usually targets middle management who are involved in planning and implementing improvements.
- **Strategic Communication**: This includes communication about the overall service strategy and how it aligns with business objectives. It's usually aimed at senior management within the organization.

In conclusion, service reporting and communication are not just about sharing numbers or broadcasting information. They are about sharing insights, sparking discussions, and making sure everyone involved in or affected by IT services has the information they need. By integrating effective service reporting and communication into your ITSM processes, you can drive continual improvement, increase satisfaction, and ensure your services deliver maximum value to the organization, aligning with the principles and requirements of ISO/IEC 20000-1.

5.4 Benchmarking and Best Practices

Benchmarking and the use of best practices are significant elements of ISO/IEC 20000-1 implementation. These practices enhance the effectiveness and efficiency of an organization's Service Management System (SMS), thereby aligning IT services with business objectives and ensuring continual improvement.

Benchmarking

Benchmarking is the process of comparing an organization's performance metrics with industry bests or best practices from other companies. In the context of ISO/IEC 20000-1, benchmarking can be used to gauge the performance of your IT services and processes, identify areas for improvement, and measure the effectiveness of improvement initiatives.

Benchmarking provides an external focus on internal activities, functions, or operations, leading to a greater understanding of best practices that, when implemented, will provide superior performance. To effectively benchmark, organizations need to:

- Identify what is to be benchmarked: the performance metrics that have a significant impact on your services.

- Identify who to benchmark against: other organizations, industry standards, or other departments within the same organization.

- Collect and analyze data: comparison data must be gathered, which requires detailed measurement and analysis.

- Implement the necessary changes: the most challenging part of the process is where strategies must be developed and executed to close the performance gap.

Best Practices

Best practices refer to the procedures and guidelines that are accepted as the most effective methods of operating in a particular area or industry. They represent the wisdom and experience accumulated by practitioners over the years and are often captured in frameworks and standards like ITIL, COBIT, and of course, ISO/IEC 20000-1 itself.

In the context of ITSM, best practices can guide organizations in areas like service strategy, design, transition, operation, and continual service improvement. Some of the reasons to adopt best practices include:

- They are based on real-world experiences and have been proven to work.

- They provide a common language and understanding, making it easier to communicate and collaborate both within and across organizations.

- They help to avoid reinventing the wheel, saving time and resources.
- They provide a basis for continual improvement, helping organizations to learn from the success of others.

However, it's important to understand that best practices should be adapted to fit the unique context of your organization. They should be seen as guidance rather than prescriptive rules.

When implemented correctly, benchmarking and the adoption of best practices can play a significant role in achieving and maintaining ISO/IEC 20000-1 compliance. They help to drive continual improvement, ensure that your services meet the needs of your customers and the business, and demonstrate that your organization is following globally recognized practices for ITSM.

In conclusion, benchmarking and best practices are integral components of ISO/IEC 20000-1. Benchmarking provides a means to gauge performance and find room for improvement. Simultaneously, best practices offer a path to navigate through the challenges that an organization may face in its journey to providing effective and efficient IT services. By using these tools, organizations can maintain a high-quality Service Management System and ensure the continual improvement of their services.

Chapter 6: Service Improvement and Continual Service Improvement (CSI)

In any organization committed to delivering high-quality IT services, the concept of improvement should never be considered a one-time effort. Instead, it should be ingrained in the organization's culture as a continuous cycle - a doctrine central to the ISO/IEC 20000-1 standard, embodied in the idea of Continual Service Improvement (CSI).

In this chapter, we will delve into the heart of Service Improvement and Continual Service Improvement, exploring the importance and the mechanics behind these concepts. We'll begin by discussing why service improvement is critical to any organization aiming to stay relevant and competitive in an ever-evolving technological landscape. From here, we'll delve into the specifics of implementing a CSI process, including various methods for identifying potential improvements and strategies to execute and measure these improvements effectively.

Next, we will take a closer look at techniques for root cause analysis and problem-solving - key methods that can help organizations prevent the recurrence of incidents and reduce the overall impact of problems. Finally, we'll explore practical steps for implementing service improvement initiatives, providing you with a roadmap for turning theoretical understanding into actionable improvement.

Whether you're new to the world of IT Service Management or an experienced professional seeking to refine your understanding, this chapter will give you valuable insights into the ongoing journey of service improvement. By the end of this chapter, you'll be equipped with a solid understanding of the principles and practices that underpin effective service improvement, along with practical strategies to embed a culture of continual improvement within your organization.

6.1 The Importance of Service Improvement

As we navigate through the digital era, the landscape of IT Service Management (ITSM) is constantly evolving. With the rapid pace of technological advancements, customer expectations and business needs are in a state of continual flux. To keep up with these changes and stay competitive, organizations must adopt a proactive approach to service improvement. By prioritizing Service Improvement, organizations can ensure they are continuously improving and adapting their services to meet changing demands, deliver value, and achieve business objectives.

Ensuring Customer Satisfaction and Loyalty

At the core of any business is its customers. Maintaining high levels of customer satisfaction and loyalty is paramount to any organization's success. However, customer expectations are not static.

As new technologies emerge and industry standards evolve, so too does what customers expect from a service.

Service Improvement ensures that an organization's services continue to meet and exceed these expectations. By continually improving and refining services, organizations can deliver better customer experiences, increasing satisfaction, fostering loyalty, and ultimately retaining more customers.

Maintaining Relevance in a Competitive Market

The IT service market is highly competitive, with numerous providers offering similar services. To differentiate from competitors and maintain relevance in the market, organizations must continuously improve and innovate their services.

Service Improvement allows organizations to regularly review their service offerings, identify areas for improvement, and innovate to provide unique value to customers. This continuous cycle of improvement and innovation helps organizations stand out in the marketplace, attract new customers, and retain existing ones.

Efficiency and Productivity Improvements

Another significant benefit of Service Improvement is increased efficiency. By regularly reviewing and improving processes, organizations can identify inefficiencies, eliminate waste, and streamline operations. This not only reduces costs but also improves the quality of services, leading to increased customer satisfaction.

Additionally, Service Improvement can boost productivity. Efficient, streamlined processes require less time and effort to execute, freeing up resources that can be allocated to other areas. Employees can focus on more valuable tasks, such as innovating new services or improving customer relationships, further enhancing the organization's overall performance.

Risk Management

In the dynamic world of IT, organizations face various risks, from data breaches and system failures to compliance issues. Service Improvement plays a vital role in mitigating these risks. Regular reviews of processes and systems can identify potential vulnerabilities and areas of non-compliance. Once identified, these issues can be addressed, reducing the risk of incidents and ensuring continued compliance with regulatory standards.

Achieving Business Objectives

Lastly, Service Improvement is essential for achieving business objectives. Whether it's increasing market share, improving profitability, or enhancing brand reputation, service improvement plays a crucial role. By continuously improving services and processes, organizations can deliver more value, attract and retain customers, and achieve their strategic objectives.

In conclusion, Service Improvement is not just a desirable element of ITSM; it's a necessity. In an ever-changing technology landscape, the organizations that will come out on top are those that embrace change, adapt, and continually strive for improvement. Through regular reviews, innovative thinking, and a commitment to continuous learning, organizations can use Service Improvement to deliver superior services, exceed customer expectations, and achieve their business objectives. Thus, the importance of Service Improvement cannot be overstated. It is the lifeblood of a thriving, competitive, and successful IT service provider.

6.2 Implementing a CSI Process

In the realm of IT Service Management, one of the critical success factors for any organization is the ability to continuously improve its services, processes, and overall performance. However, continual service improvement is not an accidental occurrence, nor does it happen in a vacuum. It requires a structured approach, codified as the Continual Service Improvement (CSI) process. Implementing a CSI process enables an organization to align its services with changing business needs, improve efficiency, increase customer satisfaction, and meet its overall strategic objectives.

Understanding the Continual Service Improvement Process

The CSI process follows a simple, cyclical model that allows organizations to consistently evaluate, benchmark, and improve their IT services. This model, often represented as the Deming Cycle or the PDCA (Plan-Do-Check-Act) cycle, includes the following steps:

i. **Plan**: Identify the need for improvement by aligning with business objectives and strategic goals. Define what should be measured, why it should be measured, and what the expected outcomes are.

ii. **Do**: Implement the improvements that were identified and planned in the previous step. This phase involves executing the action plan, which may involve changes to services, processes, tools, or infrastructure.

iii. **Check**: Monitor and measure the results of the changes implemented, and compare them against the desired outcomes defined in the planning stage.

iv. **Act**: Based on the analysis of results, make necessary adjustments to the process or service to achieve the desired outcomes. If the changes were successful, standardize them. If they were not, identify the issues, learn from them, and start the cycle again.

This cyclical model ensures that service improvement is a constant, ongoing activity and not just a one-off event.

Establishing a Continual Service Improvement Process

Implementing a CSI process involves several key steps:

Step 1: Define the Vision
Begin by clearly defining your organization's vision and strategic objectives. Understand where the business is heading and what it aims to achieve. This vision should be the guiding light for all your improvement activities.

Step 2: Assess the Current State
Analyze your organization's current situation. This involves auditing your existing IT services, processes, and capabilities to understand their effectiveness. Use this assessment to identify gaps, inefficiencies, and areas of risk.

Step 3: Prioritize Improvements
Based on the assessment, prioritize areas for improvement. Use criteria such as the potential impact on business objectives, customer satisfaction, and risk reduction to rank and prioritize improvement initiatives.

Step 4: Create a CSI Plan
Develop a detailed plan for the improvement initiatives. This should include the objectives of each initiative, the steps required, the resources needed, the metrics for success, and a timeline for implementation.

Step 5: Implement the Plan
Execute the improvement plan. Ensure that all stakeholders understand their roles and responsibilities and that the necessary resources are allocated.

Step 6: Review and Adjust
Regularly review the outcomes of the improvement initiatives. Compare actual results against expected outcomes and adjust the plan as needed. If improvements have been successful, standardize them. If not, identify issues, learn from them, and revise the plan.

Step 7: Keep the Cycle Going
Continual Service Improvement is a cyclical process. Once an improvement initiative has been completed, it's time to start the cycle again. Continually reassess your services and processes, identify new areas for improvement, and keep striving for excellence.

Cultural Considerations
Lastly, it's essential to recognize that implementing a CSI process is not just about following steps or processes; it's about fostering a culture of continual improvement. Encourage your team to continually question and challenge the status quo, learn from their mistakes, and always look for better ways of doing things. Celebrate improvements and successes, no matter how small, and encourage the sharing of ideas and feedback. This culture of continual improvement will be the driving force behind your CSI process, ensuring that your organization can adapt, grow, and succeed in the ever-evolving world of IT Service Management.

In conclusion, implementing a Continual Service Improvement process is a critical strategy for any IT service provider. It provides a structured approach to constantly enhancing service delivery, aligning services with business objectives, and achieving customer satisfaction. By continually seeking and making improvements, an organization can stay relevant, competitive, and successful in today's dynamic IT landscape.

6.3 Root Cause Analysis and Problem-Solving Techniques

In the world of IT Service Management (ITSM), problems are inevitable. However, it's the manner in which organizations deal with these problems that can make the difference between a smoothly functioning service and one fraught with recurring issues and dissatisfaction. An integral part of this process is Root Cause Analysis (RCA), a technique used to identify the underlying cause of problems.

Coupled with effective problem-solving techniques, RCA can be a powerful tool for continual service improvement.

Root Cause Analysis

At its core, Root Cause Analysis is the process of digging beneath the surface of a problem to discover the underlying cause (or causes) that led to its occurrence. The "root cause" is the deepest cause in a chain of causes and effects that leads to a problem, failure, or adverse outcome. Once identified and addressed, it prevents the issue from recurring.

RCA is not a single method or tool but a collection of different techniques and approaches. These include the Five Whys, Fishbone Diagrams (also known as Ishikawa diagrams or Cause-and-Effect diagrams), Fault Tree Analysis (FTA), and Pareto Analysis, among others.

The **Five Whys** technique, for instance, involves asking "why?" repeatedly (typically five times, though this number can vary) to trace back through the chain of events leading to the problem. It's a simple but powerful tool that helps to quickly get to the root cause of an issue.

The **Fishbone Diagram**, on the other hand, is a more visual and structured tool. It involves laying out the problem at the head of the diagram, with "bones" representing categories of potential causes. Each category is then broken down further into sub-categories and specific causes.

Fault Tree Analysis is a more advanced and systematic method used to explore and display the interrelationships among system failures. It uses a tree-like model of failures to analyze the chain of events leading to a system-level failure.

Pareto Analysis is based on the principle that 80% of problems are typically caused by 20% of the causes. It involves categorizing and ranking problems or causes to focus on the most significant ones.

Problem-Solving Techniques

While RCA helps to identify the underlying causes of problems, problem-solving techniques are then used to devise and implement solutions. These techniques provide a structured approach to address the root causes and prevent issues from recurring.

One popular problem-solving method is the **PDCA cycle (Plan-Do-Check-Act)**, also known as the Deming cycle. In the "Plan" phase, the problem and its root cause are identified, and potential solutions are devised. The "Do" phase involves implementing these solutions, while "Check" involves monitoring the effects of these changes and comparing them against the desired outcomes. Finally, in the "Act" phase, the changes are made permanent, or the cycle begins anew if the problem hasn't been resolved.

Another effective problem-solving technique is **Kepner-Tregoe problem-solving**, which provides a step-by-step approach to problem-solving. This method includes problem definition, problem analysis, decision analysis, and potential problem (opportunity) analysis.

Six Sigma's DMAIC (Define, Measure, Analyze, Improve, Control) process is also frequently used for complex problem-solving and process improvement. This technique provides a structured, data-driven approach to problem-solving and process improvement.

The Role of RCA and Problem-Solving in ITSM

In ITSM, RCA and problem-solving techniques play a crucial role in the problem management process, which aims to minimize the adverse impact of incidents and problems caused by errors within the IT infrastructure and to prevent the recurrence of these incidents.

By identifying and addressing the root causes of problems, organizations can reduce the number and severity of incidents, enhance service quality, improve customer satisfaction, and reduce costs associated with service disruptions and repairs. In essence, effective RCA and problem-solving are key to achieving and maintaining high-quality IT services.

In conclusion, Root Cause Analysis and problem-solving techniques are crucial components in IT Service Management. They are key drivers in understanding and addressing the underlying causes of problems, promoting service improvement, and ultimately, enhancing the customer experience. By incorporating these methodologies, organizations can create a more reliable, efficient, and effective IT service environment, fostering continual service improvement.

6.4 Implementing Service Improvement Initiatives

Service Improvement Initiatives (SIIs) are integral to the framework of Continual Service Improvement (CSI) in IT Service Management (ITSM). They are systematic and planned activities or projects undertaken to enhance IT service quality, operational efficiency, or business continuity. However, the journey from recognizing the need for service improvement to successfully implementing initiatives can be a challenging one. This section provides an in-depth understanding of implementing Service Improvement Initiatives effectively.

Recognizing the Need for Service Improvement

The first step in implementing service improvement initiatives is recognizing the need for improvement. There are several triggers for this recognition. It could be feedback from customers, results from satisfaction surveys, input from employees, analysis of Key Performance Indicators (KPIs), or findings from audits and reviews. The insights obtained from Root Cause Analysis of incidents and problems can also spotlight areas that need improvement.

Planning the Service Improvement Initiative

Once the need for improvement is identified, the next step is planning the initiative. Effective planning involves defining clear and measurable objectives based on the areas of improvement. This could involve improving service quality, reducing costs, enhancing customer satisfaction, or reducing the risk of service failure.

It's also essential to define the scope of the initiative. Is it a company-wide initiative or targeted at a specific department or service? What are the resources required, and what is the expected timeline? These questions need to be answered during the planning phase.

Defining Metrics and KPIs

To measure the effectiveness of a Service Improvement Initiative, it's crucial to establish relevant metrics and Key Performance Indicators (KPIs). These metrics should be directly tied to the goals of the initiative. They provide the means to evaluate progress and success and are critical in ensuring that the initiative is heading in the right direction.

Implementing the Initiative

The next step is implementing the initiative. Depending on the scope and nature of the initiative, this could involve tasks like training and development, process redesign, technological upgrades, policy changes, and more. It's important to ensure that all relevant stakeholders are on board and understand their roles and responsibilities in the initiative.

Monitoring and Review

Once the initiative is implemented, ongoing monitoring and review are necessary. The previously defined metrics and KPIs play a crucial role in this phase. Regular monitoring helps to identify any issues or bottlenecks early and allows for timely corrective action.

Periodic reviews should be carried out to assess the overall effectiveness of the initiative. These reviews can also provide insights for future improvement initiatives and contribute to an organization's continual service improvement strategy.

Challenges and Best Practices

Implementing Service Improvement Initiatives is not without its challenges. Some common obstacles include resistance to change, lack of resources, insufficient management support, and unclear objectives or KPIs.

To overcome these challenges, it's essential to involve all relevant stakeholders from the beginning and ensure clear communication throughout the process. Management support is also crucial in driving the initiative forward and overcoming resistance. Training and change management strategies can also help in preparing the workforce for the changes.

In conclusion, Service Improvement Initiatives are a critical part of Continual Service Improvement in ITSM. By identifying the need for improvement, effectively planning and implementing the initiatives, and continuously monitoring and reviewing their effectiveness, organizations can enhance their IT service delivery and achieve better business outcomes. The successful implementation of Service Improvement Initiatives not only improves the quality and efficiency of IT services, but it also enhances customer satisfaction, making it a win-win situation for all parties involved.

Chapter 7: People, Competence, and Training

The effectiveness of an organization's IT Service Management (ITSM) largely hinges upon its human resources. Technological solutions and well-designed processes are indispensable, but without skilled, competent, and motivated people to utilize these tools and execute these processes, the goals of ITSM may remain unfulfilled. This chapter, titled "People, Competence, and Training," underlines the crucial role that individuals play in the successful delivery of IT services.

In this chapter, we will delve into the various aspects of human resource management in the context of IT Service Management. We will explore the significance of competence and skills development, the role of training programs, and the importance of maintaining an engaged and motivated workforce.

We begin with an overview of human resource management in ITSM, followed by an exploration of competence frameworks and skills development. We then examine the various aspects of training and development programs, discussing how these can help nurture a highly skilled IT team that is prepared to meet the changing demands of the IT landscape.

Subsequently, we dive into the concepts of motivation, engagement, and performance management, recognizing that while technical competence is crucial, the effectiveness of an IT team also relies heavily on its level of motivation and engagement. Finally, we conclude with a discussion on the essentiality of continuous learning and development in an ever-evolving IT environment.

Each section in this chapter will provide practical advice, real-world examples, and recommendations to help you understand and implement effective strategies to develop, motivate, and manage your

IT personnel. By the end of this chapter, you should have a comprehensive understanding of the role and importance of people, competence, and training in delivering high-quality IT services in line with the ISO/IEC 20000-1 standard.

7.1 Human Resource Management in IT Service Management

The successful delivery of IT services relies heavily on the people who design, manage, and support these services. In this context, Human Resource Management (HRM) plays an integral role in IT Service Management (ITSM). Effective HRM practices are crucial in recruiting, developing, and retaining the skilled and motivated workforce required to execute ITSM processes and deliver value to customers.

Recruitment and Selection

Recruitment and selection form the first step of HRM in ITSM. It's vital to attract and select candidates with the right skills, experience, and attitude for the job. ITSM roles often require a unique combination of technical skills, problem-solving abilities, and excellent communication skills, as IT staff frequently interact with end-users and other stakeholders. Given the dynamic nature of IT, adaptability and a willingness to learn are also desirable traits.

It's also important to define clear job roles and responsibilities. The ISO/IEC 20000-1 standard requires that all individuals carrying out tasks under the service management system (SMS) be competent based on appropriate education, training, skills, and experience. Therefore, understanding the competency requirements of each role is crucial during the recruitment and selection phase.

Training and Development

Once the right individuals are onboard, training and development become crucial. Given the fast-paced evolution of technology, continuous learning is essential. IT staff needs to stay updated with the latest technologies, methodologies, and best practices. Training and development programs can range from technical skills training to soft skills development, like customer service or communication skills. In addition to external training programs, internal knowledge-sharing sessions can be an effective way of fostering continuous learning and collaboration within the team.

Performance Management
Performance management involves the continuous process of setting objectives, assessing progress, providing feedback, and making necessary adjustments to ensure that employees are meeting their performance goals. Effective performance management systems not only monitor performance but also identify areas for improvement, help in setting career development paths, and play a crucial role in recognizing and rewarding good performance.

In the context of ITSM, performance management can also involve monitoring and measuring the performance of IT services and processes and using this information to guide performance at the individual level. This could mean setting objectives related to key ITSM metrics, such as incident resolution times, customer satisfaction levels, or service availability rates.

Employee Engagement and Retention
Employee engagement and retention are key aspects of HRM in ITSM. Engaged employees are more productive, provide better service, and are more likely to stay with the organization. Factors that contribute to employee engagement include a positive work environment, opportunities for growth and development, recognition and reward for good performance, and a sense of purpose and direction.

On the other hand, high turnover rates can be detrimental to service continuity and quality. Effective retention strategies can include competitive compensation and benefits, opportunities for career advancement, a supportive work environment, and a strong organizational culture.

Compliance with ISO/IEC 20000-1

HRM practices in ITSM also need to align with the requirements of the ISO/IEC 20000-1 standard. This standard emphasizes the need for adequate resources to manage and deliver services. It also requires that all personnel working under the SMS be competent and aware of their roles and responsibilities. HRM plays a crucial role in ensuring this by recruiting competent individuals, providing necessary training, and fostering awareness and understanding of the SMS.

In conclusion, effective HRM is crucial to the successful implementation of ITSM. By recruiting the right people, providing opportunities for learning and development, implementing effective performance management systems, and fostering engagement, organizations can build a competent, motivated, and high-performing IT workforce. This, in turn, can lead to more efficient and effective IT service delivery, higher customer satisfaction levels, and improved business outcomes.

7.2 Competence Framework and Skills Development

In an era characterized by rapid technological advancements and digital transformation, the IT industry faces an ongoing challenge of developing and maintaining a workforce that is not only competent but also continuously evolves its skills to keep pace with emerging trends. This challenge highlights the importance of a well-defined competence framework and an ongoing commitment to skills development in the realm of IT Service Management (ITSM).

The Role of a Competence Framework

A competence framework, in essence, provides a structured model that defines the set of knowledge, skills, and behaviors needed to perform effectively in a particular job role or work setting. In the context of ITSM, a competence framework sets the standard for what is expected from IT professionals to successfully manage and deliver IT services.

Having a well-defined competence framework offers multiple benefits. For the organization, it helps identify gaps in existing skills and provides a roadmap for workforce planning, recruitment, and professional development. It ensures that everyone in the organization shares a common understanding of what is required to deliver high-quality IT services and how individual roles contribute to this objective.

For IT professionals, a competence framework serves as a career guide, highlighting the competencies they need to develop for their current roles and to advance their careers. It aids them in setting personal development goals and identifying the training and experiences they need to achieve these goals.

Frameworks for Competence in ITSM
Several established frameworks and methodologies provide guidance on the skills and competencies required for effective ITSM. The Information Technology Infrastructure Library (ITIL), for instance, outlines a comprehensive set of practices for ITSM and offers a robust competency model for ITSM roles.

The Skills Framework for the Information Age (SFIA) is another important resource. It provides a global language for skills and competencies in the digital world and is widely recognized across the IT industry. SFIA offers a comprehensive model of professional skills and levels of competency in various IT roles and can be a valuable tool in developing a competence framework for ITSM.

Skills Development in ITSM

Skills development is a continuous process that starts with understanding the competencies required for different roles within ITSM. Based on this understanding, organizations can design and implement various training and development programs to help IT professionals acquire and enhance these competencies.

Training programs can range from formal classroom training and online courses to on-the-job training and mentoring. They can cover a broad range of topics, from technical skills and ITSM practices to soft skills like communication, teamwork, and customer service.

Apart from training, other strategies for skills development can include providing opportunities for hands-on experiences, such as involvement in projects or rotations across different roles, promoting knowledge sharing and collaboration, and fostering a culture of continuous learning.

Aligning with ISO/IEC 20000-1 Requirements

According to the ISO/IEC 20000-1 standard, organizations are required to ensure that all personnel who carry out tasks under the service management system (SMS) are competent based on appropriate education, training, skills, and experience. They are also required to keep records of this competence.

A robust competence framework can be instrumental in meeting these requirements. By clearly defining the competencies required for different roles, it can guide recruitment, training, and development efforts to ensure that the organization has competent personnel to implement and manage the SMS.

In conclusion, a well-defined competence framework and a commitment to skills development are vital for effective ITSM. They help ensure that the IT workforce is equipped with the knowledge, skills, and behaviors needed to deliver high-quality IT services, adapt to changing needs and trends, and drive continual improvement. As such, they should be key components of any organization's ITSM strategy.

7.3 Training and Development Programs

A crucial element of implementing and maintaining a successful IT Service Management (ITSM) system under the ISO/IEC 20000-1 standard involves a focus on personnel training and development. This focus is essential for fostering competencies and skills that align with the company's service management goals. A properly designed training and development program is a tool that can support an organization's employees and lead them toward continual service improvement.

Importance of Training and Development in ITSM

The purpose of training and development in ITSM is multi-fold. Firstly, it is aimed at equipping IT service personnel with the knowledge and skills required to fulfill their roles effectively. This includes training on processes, technologies, and tools related to IT service delivery.

Secondly, training and development activities contribute to maintaining the quality of service management by ensuring that personnel remain current with the latest industry standards and practices. They also help build resilience in the workforce by preparing them to adapt to changes in the technological landscape and the evolving needs of the organization.

Furthermore, such programs contribute to employee satisfaction and retention by providing opportunities for professional growth and development. This is important because a motivated and competent workforce is key to delivering high-quality IT services and driving continuous service improvement.

Designing Effective Training and Development Programs

The design of effective training and development programs begins with an analysis of the learning needs of the workforce. This involves identifying the skills and competencies required for different roles within the ITSM framework and assessing any gaps between these requirements and the existing skills of the workforce.

In line with ISO/IEC 20000-1 requirements, training should be provided to all personnel who have a role in the service management system (SMS), including top management. This training should cover the organization's policies, procedures, and objectives related to service management, as well as the specific tasks that each individual needs to carry out as part of the SMS.

The training methodology should be chosen based on the learning objectives and the preferences and requirements of the learners. This could include classroom training, e-learning, workshops, hands-on training, and on-the-job training. It is also useful to incorporate a mix of learning methods to cater to different learning styles and ensure a more comprehensive understanding of the topics.

Assessing and Enhancing Training Effectiveness

Just as important as the delivery of training is the assessment of its effectiveness. Assessment methods can include tests, quizzes, and practical exercises to evaluate learners' understanding of the material. Feedback should be collected from participants to understand their perception of the training's relevance and usefulness.

Furthermore, organizations should monitor how the training is being applied in the workplace and its impact on service management performance. This could involve tracking key performance indicators (KPIs) related to service quality, efficiency, and customer satisfaction.

The insights gained from these assessments should be used to refine and enhance the training and development programs continually. This might involve updating the training content, improving the delivery methods, or providing additional support for learners.

Training and Development as an Ongoing Commitment
Lastly, it is important to note that training and development should not be seen as a one-time activity but as an ongoing commitment. As the field of ITSM continues to evolve, the skills and knowledge required to manage and deliver IT services effectively will also change. Therefore, organizations need to maintain a culture of continuous learning, where training and development are integral parts of the ITSM strategy.

In conclusion, well-designed training and development programs play a crucial role in implementing and maintaining an effective ITSM system under the ISO/IEC 20000-1 standard. They help equip the workforce with the necessary competencies, promote a culture of continuous learning and improvement, and ultimately contribute to better service management performance.

7.4 Motivation, Engagement, and Performance Management

A robust IT service management (ITSM) framework depends as much on the human elements involved as it does on the technical and procedural aspects. Motivation, engagement, and performance management play a crucial role in harnessing human potential and directing it toward the organization's service management goals. This chapter will explore these elements and their importance in the successful implementation of ISO/IEC 20000-1.

Motivation in ITSM

Motivation is a critical driver of human behavior and work performance. In the context of ITSM, motivation refers to the internal and external factors that stimulate employees' interest and commitment to their roles and responsibilities. Internal factors can be the inherent satisfaction one derives from the work or the sense of achievement that comes from solving complex problems or improving service quality. External factors can include financial rewards, recognition, promotions, or a positive work environment.

Understanding and harnessing these motivational factors is critical in an ITSM context, especially in the light of the ISO/IEC 20000-1 standard. A motivated workforce is more likely to embrace the organization's service management policies and procedures, strive for continual service improvement, and provide a high level of service to customers.

Engagement in ITSM

Closely related to motivation is the concept of engagement. An engaged employee is fully involved in and enthusiastic about their work. They are willing to invest discretionary effort into their work, that is, going above and beyond the basic requirements of their job to contribute to the organization's success.

Employee engagement in ITSM can be fostered in several ways. This includes creating a culture of openness and inclusivity, where employees feel valued, and their input is sought and considered in decision-making. Also, providing opportunities for growth and development, recognizing and rewarding good performance, and maintaining a healthy work-life balance are other strategies to foster engagement.

Engaged employees are likely to be more productive, deliver better customer service, and contribute positively to a collaborative and innovative work environment. This is particularly important in the context of ISO/IEC 20000-1, where employee engagement can drive the effective implementation and maintenance of the service management system (SMS).

Performance Management in ITSM

Performance management refers to the processes used by an organization to monitor, measure, and improve the performance of its employees. In ITSM, performance management includes setting clear performance expectations, regularly assessing employee performance against these expectations, providing feedback, and implementing improvement actions as needed.

A well-designed performance management system is a powerful tool for aligning individual performance with the organization's service management objectives. It provides a mechanism for identifying and addressing performance issues, recognizing and rewarding good performance, and driving continual service improvement. Furthermore, it supports compliance with ISO/IEC 20000-1, which requires the organization to demonstrate effective performance management as part of its SMS.

Integrating Motivation, Engagement, and Performance Management in ITSM

Motivation, engagement, and performance management are not standalone concepts, but rather they are intertwined and mutually reinforcing. Motivated and engaged employees are likely to perform better, and effective performance management can, in turn, boost motivation and engagement by providing clear expectations, timely feedback, and recognition of good performance.

Therefore, organizations aiming to comply with ISO/IEC 20000-1 should integrate these concepts into their ITSM strategy. This might involve incorporating motivation and engagement strategies into the organization's human resource policies, linking performance management to training and development activities, and aligning all these elements with the organization's service management objectives.

Furthermore, it's essential to measure and monitor these aspects regularly using suitable metrics. For instance, employee surveys can be used to assess motivation and engagement levels, while key performance indicators (KPIs) can be used to measure various aspects of performance. These metrics can provide valuable insights for improving the organization's ITSM practices and achieving compliance with ISO/IEC 20000-1.

In conclusion, motivation, engagement, and performance management are critical elements of a successful ITSM framework. By focusing on these aspects, organizations can create a work environment that fosters a commitment to service excellence, drives continual service improvement, and supports compliance with ISO/IEC 20000-1.

Chapter 8: Technology and Tooling for Service Management

As we traverse the digital landscape, the significance of technology and tooling in IT service management (ITSM) can hardly be overstated. The 8th chapter of our journey through "Mastering ISO/IEC 20000-1" emphasizes the role of these elements in the effective implementation and execution of ITSM processes. As a component of ISO/IEC 20000-1 standard, these factors play a pivotal role in building a robust, compliant, and efficient Service Management System (SMS).

This chapter will take you through the key technologies and tools that are fundamental to achieving superior service management. We'll start with an overview of service management tools and their potential for automation, moving onto specific categories of tools such as Configuration Management Databases (CMDBs), Incident and Problem Management tools, Change and Release Management tools, and Performance Monitoring and Reporting tools.

We will explore how these technologies can streamline operations, bolster process efficiency, and provide in-depth insights into service performance. Additionally, we'll delve into how the judicious application of these tools can empower organizations to align their ITSM operations with the broader business strategy, thereby driving growth and sustainability.

This chapter aims to provide you with a comprehensive understanding of how to leverage technology in the pursuit of ITSM excellence. Regardless of whether you're an IT professional seeking to enhance your technical knowledge, or a business leader wanting to grasp how technology can enhance service management, this chapter promises to provide practical insights and guidance.

8.1 Service Management Tools and Automation

The rapid digitization and complex nature of today's business environment have led to an exponential increase in the demand for effective IT service management (ITSM). This is where service management tools and automation come in, helping to simplify, streamline, and enhance ITSM processes.

Service management tools are software solutions designed to assist organizations in planning, delivering, operating, and controlling IT services provided to customers. They often form the backbone of ITSM operations, supporting various processes, from incident and problem management to change and configuration management.

One crucial aspect of service management tools is their capacity for automation. Automation in ITSM is the use of technology to perform recurring tasks or processes in a business where manual effort can be replaced. It is deployed to minimize costs, increase efficiency, and streamline processes. The application of automation technologies not only leads to operational efficiency but also reduces the likelihood of human error, a factor that can often result in system vulnerabilities and service interruptions.

Service management tools encompass a wide range of software solutions, including ticketing systems, IT asset management tools, customer relationship management systems, knowledge management platforms, and reporting and analytics tools. They can handle tasks ranging from managing service requests, incidents, and problems, to overseeing change requests, managing IT assets, and maintaining service level agreements (SLAs).

To illustrate the value of these tools, let's consider an example. Suppose an IT department receives a high volume of service requests each day. Without a suitable service management tool in place, tracking, prioritizing, and resolving these requests can quickly become unmanageable. However, with an ITSM tool, these requests can be easily logged, assigned, tracked, and resolved while providing the IT team with visibility into the status of each request.

Automating service management processes can deliver a host of benefits. First, it can significantly improve efficiency by reducing the time and effort required to manage tasks. For instance, instead of manually logging and assigning tickets, an ITSM tool can automate these tasks based on predefined rules, allowing IT staff to focus on more complex issues.

Second, automation can enhance service quality. By automating routine tasks, organizations can minimize human error, ensure consistency in how tasks are performed, and improve their response time to service requests. Additionally, ITSM tools often include features for tracking and managing SLAs, ensuring that service delivery meets agreed-upon standards.

Third, automation can improve visibility and control over ITSM processes. Most ITSM tools include reporting and analytics features, providing IT teams with valuable insights into their operations. This can aid in identifying bottlenecks, tracking performance against KPIs, and making informed decisions to improve service delivery.

However, while automation can deliver significant benefits, it's essential to approach it strategically. Not all tasks are suitable for automation; trying to automate complex tasks that require human judgment could lead to poor results. Therefore, organizations should focus on automating repetitive, routine tasks that don't require critical thinking.

Furthermore, successful automation requires careful planning and management. This includes defining clear goals for automation, selecting the right tools, integrating them with existing systems, and training staff to use them effectively. It's also crucial to monitor and continually improve automation initiatives to ensure they deliver the expected benefits.

In conclusion, service management tools and automation are essential components of effective ITSM. By leveraging these technologies, organizations can enhance their efficiency, improve service quality, and gain valuable insights into their operations. However, to fully realize these benefits, organizations must approach automation strategically, ensuring that it aligns with their ITSM objectives and capabilities.

8.2 Configuration Management Databases (CMDBs)

The Configuration Management Database (CMDB) serves as the bedrock of any robust IT Service Management (ITSM) strategy. Acting as a dynamic information repository, a CMDB encapsulates an organization's IT infrastructure, housing essential data related to all configuration items (CIs) within the network.

Configuration items can range from computing hardware, such as servers, routers, and workstations, to software applications and network configurations and even encompass service data and documentation. Essentially, any component that has a role in the delivery of an IT service can be a CI. Each CI's characteristics, interrelationships, and dependencies on other CIs are meticulously documented in the CMDB, providing a bird's eye view of the organization's IT landscape.

Having a unified and dynamic resource like a CMDB offers many strategic advantages for an organization striving to comply with ISO/IEC 20000-1 and other ITSM best practices. One of the most significant benefits is the ability to track and manage all aspects of a CI across its lifecycle. From the point of acquisition or creation through to disposal or retirement, every state change, update, or modification to a CI is recorded in the CMDB, fostering improved governance and operational control.

By mapping dependencies between CIs, a CMDB aids in impact analysis and risk management. When a change is proposed, or an incident occurs, the IT team can refer to the CMDB to understand the potential knock-on effects. This leads to informed decision-making, minimizing the risk of disruptions to services and enhancing the speed and efficiency of incident and problem management processes.

Moreover, a well-implemented CMDB supports configuration management, a vital ITSM process mandated by ISO/IEC 20000-1. It provides a single source of truth about the organization's IT environment, enabling the IT team to plan and manage changes more effectively, ensure the integrity and consistency of CIs, and validate that the actual IT environment aligns with what's recorded.

Despite these benefits, implementing a CMDB is not a trivial task. It requires careful planning, a deep understanding of the organization's IT environment, and ongoing management to ensure that the CMDB remains accurate and up-to-date.

The initial configuration of the CMDB begins with defining the scope of CIs to be included. This involves identifying the various types of CIs in the organization, outlining the attributes to be recorded for each CI, and determining how CIs are interrelated. The accuracy of this initial configuration has a direct bearing on the value derived from the CMDB.

Post-implementation, it's essential to ensure the CMDB remains accurate, up-to-date, and reflective of the organization's dynamic IT environment. This necessitates robust processes for adding new CIs, updating CI attributes when changes occur, and removing CIs when they are retired or disposed of. Periodic audits and reviews of the CMDB can help ensure its integrity, helping it remain a valuable tool for ITSM.

Furthermore, implementing a CMDB does not exist in a vacuum. It should be aligned with other ITSM processes, such as change management, incident management, and service level management, to ensure cohesive, efficient operations.

In conclusion, a CMDB, while complex to implement and manage, is a powerful tool in the arsenal of any organization committed to effective ITSM. It facilitates better decision-making, risk management, and IT governance, driving value across various ITSM processes. Therefore, investing in a CMDB and the resources necessary to maintain it is essential for an organization aiming to adhere to ISO/IEC 20000-1 and other ITSM best practices.

8.3 Incident and Problem Management Tools

Incident and problem management are core processes of any effective IT Service Management (ITSM) strategy, playing crucial roles in maintaining the availability and quality of IT services. These processes are supported by a variety of specialized tools that not only facilitate their execution but also align them with the best practices outlined in standards like ISO/IEC 20000-1.

An incident management tool is designed to record, track, and manage incidents—defined as any disruption or degradation in the quality of an IT service. The tool enables IT support teams to log incidents, assign them to the appropriate personnel, monitor their status, and ultimately ensure their timely resolution. Most tools also provide functionalities such as automated alerts, reporting features, and integrations with other systems for seamless information flow.

A key aspect of incident management tools is their ability to categorize and prioritize incidents. This ensures that high-impact incidents affecting multiple users or critical services receive attention first. The tool also maintains a historical record of all incidents, which can be invaluable for future incident analysis, identifying recurring issues, and improving service delivery.

On the other hand, a problem management tool aims to identify and eliminate the root causes of recurring or significant incidents. It supports the logging, categorization, investigation, and resolution of problems, as well as the implementation of preventative measures. These tools often include capabilities for tracking known errors and maintaining a knowledge base which houses solutions to common problems, assisting in faster resolution times and reducing the strain on IT support teams.

It's essential to note that while incident management focuses on restoring service operations as quickly as possible, problem management seeks to identify and rectify the underlying issues causing the incidents. Consequently, the tools supporting these processes, while interconnected, have different focuses and functionalities.

In a well-integrated ITSM system, incident and problem management tools should be closely linked. An ongoing incident might trigger a problem record or a known error in the problem database might suggest a resolution for a new incident.

Advanced incident and problem management tools offer features beyond the basics. Automation is becoming increasingly prevalent, with capabilities such as auto-assignment of incidents based on predefined rules, automated escalation of incidents or problems if they're not addressed within a certain timeframe or even automated resolution of certain common incidents.

Furthermore, contemporary tools incorporate functionalities like chatbots and virtual agents that leverage Artificial Intelligence (AI) and Natural Language Processing (NLP) to interact with users in a human-like manner. They can resolve common incidents without human intervention, freeing up support staff to handle more complex issues.

In terms of alignment with the ISO/IEC 20000-1 standard, these tools can play a significant role. They can demonstrate effective incident and problem management processes, provide evidence for audits, and support continual improvement by providing data for analysis and trend identification.

Moreover, they support other ISO/IEC 20000-1 requirements, such as customer communication (by keeping users informed about the status of their incidents) and service continuity management (by enabling rapid response to incidents that could result in service outages).

Investing in the right incident and problem management tools can significantly enhance an organization's ability to meet its ITSM objectives. However, it's important to remember that tools are just part of the equation. They must be coupled with well-designed processes, skilled personnel, and a culture of service excellence to realize their full potential. When all these elements come together, organizations can not only meet the requirements of ISO/IEC 20000-1 but also improve service quality, reduce downtime, and increase customer satisfaction.

8.4 Change and Release Management Tools

Change and release management are critical elements of the IT service management (ITSM) lifecycle, playing crucial roles in ensuring that IT services evolve to meet business needs while minimizing disruption to services. Like other ITSM processes, they are supported by various tools that are designed to facilitate their execution and align them with best practices, including those outlined in standards like ISO/IEC 20000-1.

Change management tools aid in the systematic approach to handling changes in an IT infrastructure. The primary function of these tools is to ensure that standardized methods and procedures are used for efficient and prompt handling of all changes, reducing the risk of negatively impacting service quality.

From the moment a change is proposed through the assessment, authorization, implementation, and review stages, change management tools enable tracking, control, and validation of changes. They offer capabilities such as automated workflows, which ensure that each change follows the right steps in the right order; a change schedule (also known as a Forward Schedule of Change), which helps avoid conflicts between changes; and a historical record of all changes, which aids in review and audit processes.

Moreover, advanced change management tools incorporate features such as impact analysis, which can predict the effects of a proposed change on services and other configuration items (CIs), and integration with configuration management tools, which provides the necessary context for assessing changes.

Release management tools, on the other hand, help manage the process of planning, scheduling, and controlling the movement of releases to test and live environments. They ensure that all software and hardware changes to the IT infrastructure are released properly and consistently.

The functionalities offered by release management tools include managing the release calendar (to plan and schedule releases); controlling the release package's components (including software, hardware, and associated documentation); verifying that the release is built, installed, and tested consistently; and ensuring that new or changed services are capable of delivering the intended outcomes.

A significant feature of contemporary release management tools is their ability to automate various aspects of the release process. From automating the building and deployment of releases to testing and validation of the release, these tools can greatly enhance the speed, efficiency, and accuracy of the release process.

In an integrated ITSM system, change and release management tools should be closely connected. Changes that are authorized should feed into the release management process, and successful releases might close associated change records.

The role of these tools in supporting ISO/IEC 20000-1 compliance is significant. They provide an auditable trail of changes and releases, demonstrating that the organization has control over these processes. They also support other requirements of the standard, such as service continuity (by reducing the risk of disruptive changes) and service reporting (by providing data on the success rate of changes and releases).

In the context of contemporary IT practices such as DevOps and Agile, which emphasize rapid and frequent changes, the role of change and release management tools becomes even more critical. They can enable organizations to strike a balance between the speed of delivery and the stability of services – a balance that is at the heart of ISO/IEC 20000-1 and ITSM in general.

In summary, while investing in change and release management tools are important, organizations should remember that successful change and release management also depends on well-designed and well-executed processes, skilled and knowledgeable people, and a culture that supports and values these practices. When these elements are combined with effective tools, organizations can meet their ITSM objectives and deliver services that meet business needs while minimizing disruption and risk.

8.5 Performance Monitoring and Reporting Tools

Performance monitoring and reporting tools are crucial elements in the IT service management (ITSM) toolbox. They provide the ability to measure, track, analyze, and report on various aspects of IT service performance, supporting decision-making and continuous improvement activities. This underpins many of the requirements of standards like ISO/IEC 20000-1, which emphasize the importance of evidence-based decision-making and continual improvement of services.

Performance monitoring tools collect data on the technical performance of IT infrastructure components like servers, network devices, applications, and services. They can provide real-time information on a wide range of metrics, such as processor utilization, memory usage, network latency, transaction times, and error rates. This information can help identify problems before they impact service quality and provide insight into capacity and availability trends, supporting capacity management and service continuity processes.

Furthermore, advanced performance monitoring tools may offer features such as predictive analytics, which use historical data and statistical models to forecast future performance trends. This can provide early warnings of potential problems, allowing proactive measures to be taken. Another feature offered by some tools is baseline comparison, which compares current performance to a previously established 'normal' level, identifying any significant deviations.

The functionality of performance monitoring tools often extends to incident detection and alerting, sending notifications to relevant personnel or systems when certain thresholds are exceeded. This can trigger incident management processes, reducing the time taken to respond to and resolve incidents.

Performance reporting tools, on the other hand, focus on processing and presenting the data collected by performance monitoring tools and other sources. They can aggregate data from multiple sources, providing a consolidated view of performance across the entire IT service landscape. This is especially important in complex, multi-vendor environments where services depend on components provided by different suppliers.

Performance reports provide the evidence needed to make informed decisions on service improvement, capacity planning, supplier management, and other key ITSM processes. They can also provide evidence of compliance with service level agreements (SLAs) and other performance targets, supporting service level management and customer relationship management processes.

Effective performance reporting tools should offer features such as customizable dashboards, which allow users to select and arrange the metrics that are most relevant to them, and automated report generation and distribution, which ensure that stakeholders receive timely and accurate performance information. They should also support trend analysis, enabling changes in performance over time to be identified and understood.

In the context of ISO/IEC 20000-1, performance monitoring and reporting tools provide crucial support for several requirements of the standard. They support the establishment and management of SLAs (by providing evidence of service performance) and the identification and resolution of incidents (by detecting and alerting performance issues). They also support the continual improvement of services (by providing data on current performance and trends) and the management of suppliers (by providing evidence of supplier performance).

In a world where IT services are becoming increasingly complex and dynamic and where customer expectations are continually rising, the role of performance monitoring and reporting tools in ITSM cannot be overstated. They provide the data and insights needed to understand and manage service performance, anticipate and respond to performance issues, and continually improve services to meet evolving business needs.

However, like other ITSM tools, their effectiveness depends not only on their technical capabilities but also on the processes, people, and culture of the organization. Properly configured and used, and supported by effective processes and skilled people, these tools can help an organization achieve its ITSM objectives and meet the requirements of ISO/IEC 20000-1.

Chapter 9: Service Integration and Management (SIAM)

Chapter 9 dives into the intricacies of Service Integration and Management (SIAM), a methodology that has grown increasingly important in modern IT Service Management (ITSM). As IT environments have evolved to become more complex and multi-vendor oriented, managing and integrating various service providers and their services into a cohesive, unified ecosystem has become critical. SIAM offers a governance framework that orchestrates this complicated dance of service providers to deliver seamless, efficient, and high-quality IT services.

In this chapter, we will unravel the core principles and concepts of SIAM, shedding light on its purpose and role within the realm of ITSM. We will explore how to effectively implement SIAM within a multi-sourced environment, from setting up governance structures to defining clear roles and responsibilities among diverse service providers.

Moreover, we will delve into SIAM's distinct integration models, offering a comprehensive understanding of how these models can be leveraged to manage relationships and align various service components. We will also present the challenges that often surface in SIAM implementation and provide practical solutions, coupled with best practices, to navigate these hurdles successfully.

Through this chapter, readers will gain an in-depth understanding of SIAM and its inherent role in enhancing service delivery in line with the ISO/IEC 20000-1 standard. Let's embark on this journey to master the orchestration of multi-vendor IT service landscapes with SIAM.

9.1 Understanding SIAM Principles and Concepts

Service Integration and Management (SIAM) is a methodological framework that governs multiple service providers and integrates them to provide a single, business-focused IT organization. As IT services become increasingly diversified and delivered through various channels, SIAM becomes essential to ensure that all these diverse parts move together cohesively towards a shared goal.

SIAM is based on several principles and concepts that establish a structure and roadmap for managing multiple service providers effectively. The key principles of SIAM are:

1. Business alignment: This is one of the cornerstones of SIAM, where IT services are aligned with the business objectives and goals. SIAM stresses the importance of a business-oriented approach, where all service providers understand the organization's strategic goals and align their services accordingly.

2. Supplier management: SIAM emphasizes the importance of managing all suppliers as integrated parts of the IT services, rather than separate entities. This includes effective management of contracts, relationships, and performance of the service providers.

3. Standardization: SIAM promotes the use of standardized processes and procedures across all service providers. This ensures consistency in service delivery and makes the integration of services easier and more efficient.

4. Integration: The fundamental concept of SIAM is to integrate various IT service providers into a unified, coherent service delivery framework. This involves integrating processes, tools, data, and people from various service providers to deliver seamless IT services.

5. Governance: SIAM provides a governance framework that ensures all service providers adhere to the defined standards, processes, and performance metrics. This framework also ensures accountability and transparency in service delivery.

6. End-to-end service visibility: SIAM emphasizes the need for a holistic view of IT services, from end to end. This means considering the entire service lifecycle, from the initial design and planning to the operation, monitoring, and continual improvement of services.

7. Collaboration: A successful SIAM framework fosters a culture of collaboration and mutual respect among service providers. This ensures that all providers work towards a shared goal of providing the best service to the business.

Now, let's delve into some essential SIAM concepts.

The **SIAM ecosystem** refers to the entire landscape of service providers, their relationships, integrated services, processes, tools, and governance structures. This ecosystem must be well-orchestrated to deliver the seamless service delivery that SIAM aims for.

The **Service Integrator** plays a key role in SIAM, responsible for integrating and coordinating the services of multiple service providers. The Service Integrator ensures that all providers adhere to the defined processes, meet the performance metrics, and work collaboratively to deliver IT services.

Service towers are another crucial concept in SIAM. They represent the functional areas of IT services, such as infrastructure, application development, or network services. Each tower may be managed by a different service provider but must be coordinated and integrated under the Service Integrator's leadership.

The **SIAM roadmap** provides a step-by-step guide to implementing SIAM in an organization. It outlines the stages of SIAM adoption, from the initial assessment of the current situation, through the design and implementation of SIAM, to the continual improvement of the SIAM framework.

In conclusion, understanding these principles and concepts is foundational to leveraging SIAM effectively in managing multiple service providers. In the next sections, we'll delve deeper into how to implement SIAM in a multisourced environment, explore different SIAM governance and integration models, and discuss the challenges and best practices in SIAM implementation. As we progress, you'll appreciate even more the role that these principles and concepts play in shaping a successful SIAM framework.

9.2 Implementing SIAM in a Multi-sourced Environment

The growing complexity and diversity of IT services demand a strategic approach to manage them cohesively. A multi-sourced IT environment involves various service providers delivering different IT services. Service Integration and Management (SIAM) offers a robust framework that ensures seamless service delivery by integrating these disparate services into a single, well-managed entity. Implementing SIAM in such an environment can be quite challenging, but it provides immense benefits when done effectively. In this section, we'll discuss the process of implementing SIAM in a multi-sourced environment.

Initial Assessment:

Before embarking on the SIAM journey, it's essential to conduct an initial assessment of the current IT service management environment. This involves reviewing the existing service management processes, identifying the various service providers, evaluating their performance, understanding the nature and scope of their services, and assessing the level of integration and collaboration among them. This assessment provides a baseline from which to design the SIAM model and helps identify potential obstacles that might hinder SIAM implementation.

Designing the SIAM Model:

Based on the initial assessment, an organization can design its SIAM model. This involves defining the SIAM principles and policies, designing the SIAM governance structure, identifying service towers, and appointing the service integrator.

Service towers are significant IT functional areas, such as infrastructure, applications, security, etc., each possibly managed by a different service provider. The service integrator role is crucial for coordinating and integrating these service towers. Depending on the organization's preference, the service integrator role can be internal or outsourced to a third-party provider.

Implementation and Transition:
Once the SIAM model is designed, the next step is to implement it. This involves transitioning from the current IT service management model to the SIAM model. During this phase, organizations should ensure that all service providers understand the SIAM model, principles, and their roles and responsibilities.

The existing processes may need to be re-engineered or adapted to fit the SIAM model, and new processes may need to be introduced. Furthermore, necessary tools and technologies should be put in place to support SIAM implementation, such as service management tools, integration tools, and performance monitoring tools.

Service Integration:
Service integration is the core of SIAM, where all services from different providers are integrated to provide a unified IT service. The service integrator plays a crucial role in this phase, ensuring seamless integration and collaboration among all service providers. This involves integrating processes, data, tools, and ensuring clear communication and coordination among all parties.

Performance Monitoring and Continual Improvement:
Once SIAM is implemented, the organization should continuously monitor its performance. This involves tracking key performance indicators (KPIs), measuring service levels, and assessing customer satisfaction. These metrics should be aligned with the organization's

business objectives and should provide insights into the effectiveness of the SIAM model.

Based on performance monitoring, organizations should strive for continual improvement of the SIAM model. This involves identifying areas of improvement, implementing corrective measures, and regularly reviewing the SIAM model to ensure its effectiveness.

Implementing SIAM in a multi-sourced environment is not without challenges. These may include resistance to change, communication issues, discrepancies in processes among service providers, and maintaining service quality during the transition to SIAM. However, with a well-planned approach, strong leadership, and effective communication, these challenges can be managed effectively.

In conclusion, SIAM provides a comprehensive framework for managing multiple service providers in an integrated manner. When implemented effectively, it enhances service quality, improves service coordination, provides better control over IT services, and ensures alignment with business objectives. The journey to SIAM may be challenging, but the benefits it offers make it worth the effort.

9.3 SIAM Governance and Integration Models

Governance is a critical aspect of Service Integration and Management (SIAM) as it ensures effective control, coordination, and management of various service providers involved in delivering IT services. Similarly, the integration model is fundamental to the operation of SIAM, as it determines how various service providers' processes, tools, and data will be integrated to ensure seamless service delivery. In this section, we will explore the facets of SIAM governance and integration models.

SIAM Governance

The governance structure in a SIAM ecosystem is pivotal in defining and enforcing policies, procedures, roles, and responsibilities across the multiple service providers. A well-established governance framework ensures standardized service management, accountability, and transparency in delivering IT services.

1. Defining the Governance Structure

The first step in establishing SIAM governance is to define a robust governance structure. This structure should be hierarchically designed, starting from strategic, through tactical, down to the operational level. The top layer involves the strategic decision-makers, including the Chief Information Officer (CIO) and other top executives. The middle layer consists of service managers, while the lower layer comprises operational teams from different service providers.

2. Roles and Responsibilities

A clear definition of roles and responsibilities is crucial in SIAM governance. These roles can include the service integrator, service owner, process owner, service provider, and business relationship manager, among others. Each role should have clear responsibilities, deliverables, and reporting lines defined.

3. Governance Processes and Mechanisms

SIAM governance encompasses a range of processes and mechanisms to manage the service providers and their services effectively. These may include service level management, risk management, compliance management, contract management, performance management, and more. The governance mechanisms can include regular meetings, reporting structures, performance dashboards, audit mechanisms, and more.

4. Policies and Procedures

Effective SIAM governance also involves creating and enforcing policies and procedures that all service providers must adhere to. These policies could relate to service delivery, performance reporting, risk management, and information security, among other areas. These policies and procedures help ensure standardization and consistency across all service providers.

SIAM Integration Models

While the governance model ensures effective management and control of service providers, the integration model ensures that the services provided by these different providers are seamlessly integrated to deliver a unified IT service.

1. Service Integration

The integration model should ensure that the services delivered by different service providers are integrated seamlessly. This involves integrating service management processes, tools, and data across the service providers. The service integrator plays a crucial role in this integration, acting as a glue that binds all the services together.

2. Process Integration

Process integration involves aligning and integrating the service management processes across different service providers. This may involve re-engineering some processes, aligning processes to industry best practices, and introducing new processes where needed.

3. Tool Integration

In a SIAM environment, service providers may use different tools for managing their services. The integration model should ensure that these tools are integrated, allowing data and information to flow seamlessly across them. This may involve tool consolidation, tool integration, or the use of an overlay tool that integrates data from different tools.

4. Data Integration

Data integration involves integrating and consolidating data from different service providers to provide a unified view of service performance. This enables effective performance monitoring, decision-making, and reporting.

In conclusion, both governance and integration models play vital roles in a SIAM environment. While the governance model ensures effective control and management of service providers, the integration model ensures seamless integration of services, processes, tools, and data across service providers. Both these models should be designed and implemented carefully, considering the organization's context, the nature of the services, and the service providers involved.

9.4 Challenges and Best Practices in SIAM Implementation

Implementing Service Integration and Management (SIAM) in a multi-sourced IT service environment is no small feat. It involves the management and orchestration of multiple service providers to deliver a seamless and unified IT service to the business. In this chapter, we will explore some of the key challenges encountered during SIAM implementation and share some best practices to navigate these challenges effectively.

Challenges in SIAM Implementation

There are several challenges that organizations may encounter during the implementation of SIAM. Here are some of the most common ones:

1. Lack of Clear Governance: One of the primary challenges in SIAM implementation is the absence of a clear governance structure. With multiple service providers, managing roles, responsibilities, and accountability becomes a daunting task.

2. Integration Issues: The integration of processes, tools, and data across multiple service providers is another significant challenge. Each service provider may have its unique processes and tools, making integration difficult.

3. Resistance to Change: The transition to a SIAM model is a significant change for many organizations. This change may encounter resistance from both the organization and the service providers, which can stall or even derail the implementation process.

4. Performance Measurement: Measuring the performance of multiple service providers in a unified manner is challenging. Defining common

Key Performance Indicators (KPIs) and service level agreements (SLAs) across diverse service providers can be complex.

5. Cultural Differences: The diverse cultures of different service providers can pose a challenge to SIAM implementation. These differences can affect communication, teamwork, and overall service delivery.

Best Practices in SIAM Implementation

Despite these challenges, several best practices can make SIAM implementation more manageable and successful. Here are some of them:

1. Define Clear Governance: Establish a robust governance structure with clearly defined roles, responsibilities, and accountability. This structure should cover the strategic, tactical, and operational levels of the organization.

2. Use a Phased Approach: SIAM implementation is a significant transformation. Instead of trying to achieve it all at once, use a phased approach. This method allows for learning and adjustment at each phase before moving to the next.

3. Invest in Integration Tools: Deploy tools that can facilitate the integration of processes, data, and other tools across service providers. Such tools can automate many integration tasks, reducing complexity and saving time.

4. Change Management: Address resistance to change by investing in change management. This involves communicating the benefits of SIAM, training staff, and involving them in the implementation process to gain their buy-in.

5. Define Common KPIs and SLAs: Define a set of common KPIs and SLAs that apply to all service providers. This allows for consistent performance measurement and management across providers.

6. Cultural Integration: Cultural differences among service providers should be addressed upfront. Organize team-building activities and communication sessions to bring different teams together and build a unified culture.

7. Continuous Improvement: Once SIAM is implemented, continuously monitor and improve it. Use performance data to identify areas of improvement and implement corrective actions.

In conclusion, while SIAM implementation is challenging, it is feasible with a clear strategy, robust governance, and continuous improvement. By addressing integration issues, managing change, and overcoming cultural differences, organizations can realize the benefits of SIAM and deliver seamless IT service to their businesses.

Chapter 10: Service Management and Business Relationship Management

Chapter 10 delves into the pivotal role of Service Management and Business Relationship Management in organizations. As IT service management continues to evolve, its alignment with business objectives becomes increasingly important. This alignment is achieved through effective Business Relationship Management (BRM).

In this chapter, we explore how IT services can be effectively aligned with business objectives, fostering a symbiotic relationship that drives mutual growth and success. We will delve into the ways in which IT organizations can build effective relationships with business stakeholders, enhance customer satisfaction, manage service experiences, and contribute meaningfully to business-IT alignment and value creation.

It's crucial to note that strong business relationships don't just happen—they are built through a consistent, value-driven approach. They require regular and open communication, a clear understanding of the needs and objectives of both sides and a commitment to delivering tangible business benefits.

As we navigate through this chapter, you'll gain a deeper understanding of the practices, techniques, and strategies needed to create strong, value-driven relationships between IT service management and business stakeholders, enhancing overall business performance and success.

10.1 Aligning IT Services with Business Objectives

One of the central tenets of effective IT Service Management (ITSM) is aligning IT services with the business objectives. This principle requires an understanding of not just the mechanics of IT services but also the broader strategic context of the organization. In this section, we will explore what this alignment means, why it's critical, and how organizations can achieve it.

IT services, whether in-house or sourced externally, are essential enablers of business functions. Whether it's supporting internal communication, managing customer relationships, or driving data analytics, IT services are integral to a business's performance and strategic objectives. In this respect, IT is not just an operational necessity but a strategic partner.

Aligning IT services with business objectives means ensuring that IT services not only support but also enable and drive the achievement of these objectives. This alignment is not a one-time event but an ongoing process that should be continually monitored, assessed, and adjusted.

A central aspect of achieving alignment is understanding the strategic context. IT service managers need to understand the business strategy, goals, and objectives. This understanding includes awareness of the company's competitive position, market dynamics, customer expectations, regulatory requirements, and other factors that shape the business strategy.

Once the business context is understood, the IT service strategy can be developed to support and enable the strategic objectives. For example, if a business aims to expand into new markets, the IT service strategy might focus on developing the capabilities to support this expansion, such as scalability or localization features.

This strategic alignment requires open and ongoing communication between IT and business leadership. Regular strategic reviews should be conducted to ensure alignment, identify emerging needs, and adjust the strategy as needed.

However, aligning IT services with business objectives isn't only about strategy. It's also about execution. This execution involves designing and delivering IT services that meet the needs of the business. It means understanding the business processes that the services support, the end-users of the services, and the performance and quality requirements.

Effective IT service design and transition processes are critical for ensuring that services are fit for purpose and fit for use. Service Level Agreements (SLAs) should be defined to set clear expectations for service performance and quality. Regular service reviews should be conducted to monitor performance, identify improvement opportunities, and ensure the continued alignment of the services with the evolving business needs.

Aligning IT services with business objectives also involves demonstrating the value of IT. Often, the value of IT services isn't fully recognized by the business. IT service managers need to be able to quantify and communicate the value delivered by their services in terms that the business understands. This might involve demonstrating how IT services increase efficiency, reduce costs, improve customer satisfaction, or enable new business opportunities.

In conclusion, aligning IT services with business objectives is a strategic necessity for any business. It involves understanding the business context, developing a service strategy that supports the business objectives, designing and delivering services that meet the needs of the business, and demonstrating the value of these services. It requires strong communication, strategic thinking, service management expertise, and a commitment to continuous improvement. By aligning IT services with business objectives, organizations can ensure that IT is a strategic partner that contributes to the achievement of business success.

10.2 Building Effective Relationships with Business Stakeholders

In the modern business environment, the alignment of IT services with business objectives requires building effective relationships with business stakeholders. This notion goes beyond mere consultation or communication - it involves fostering a collaborative partnership where both sides understand, respect, and support each other's roles, goals, and contributions. In this section, we'll discuss the importance of these relationships, who these stakeholders might be, and strategies for building strong, mutually beneficial partnerships.

The nature of IT services makes them inherently cross-functional. They support almost all areas of the business, interact with multiple processes, and affect a wide range of stakeholders. These stakeholders may include internal users, business unit managers, executives, and even external entities such as customers or suppliers. Each stakeholder has unique needs, expectations, and perspectives on IT services.

Building effective relationships with these stakeholders is critical for several reasons. Firstly, it helps ensure that IT services truly meet the needs of the business. By engaging with stakeholders, IT service managers can gain a deeper understanding of their needs, expectations, and pain points. This understanding allows them to design and deliver services that are fit for purpose and fit for use.

Secondly, these relationships facilitate alignment between IT and the business. Through regular interaction and communication, IT service managers can keep a pulse on the strategic direction of the business, emerging needs, and changes in the business environment. This information helps them ensure that the IT service strategy remains aligned with the business objectives.

Thirdly, these relationships help improve the perception and value of IT within the business. By building strong relationships, IT service managers can demonstrate their understanding of the business, their commitment to serving its needs, and the value that their services bring. This visibility can enhance the reputation of IT, elevate its role within the business, and facilitate the securing of resources and support.

Building these relationships, however, requires deliberate effort and strategies. Here are some strategies that IT service managers can employ:

i. **Stakeholder Identification and Analysis:** Not all stakeholders are created equal. IT service managers should identify their key stakeholders and analyze their interests, influence, and expectations. This analysis helps them understand who to engage with, how to approach them, and what issues to address.

ii. **Regular Communication:** Effective communication is the bedrock of any relationship. IT service managers should establish regular communication channels with stakeholders, such as meetings, reports, or newsletters. These channels should be used to update stakeholders about service performance, upcoming changes, and other relevant information, as well as to gather feedback and input.

iii. **Involvement in Decision-Making:** Involve stakeholders in decision-making processes related to IT services. This might include service design, priority setting, or problem resolution. Involvement increases stakeholders' sense of ownership and commitment to the services.

iv. **Relationship-Building Activities:** In addition to formal communication and collaboration, IT service managers should engage in activities that build personal relationships with stakeholders. This might include informal meetings, social events, or team-building activities.

v. **Manage Expectations:** Make sure to manage stakeholder expectations effectively. This includes setting clear service level agreements (SLAs), communicating regularly about service performance, and addressing any gaps between expected and actual service levels promptly and transparently.

vi. **Demonstrate Value:** Continuously demonstrate the value that IT services bring to the business. This might involve showcasing success stories, quantifying the benefits of services, or highlighting the role of IT in enabling business achievements.

In conclusion, building effective relationships with business stakeholders is a critical aspect of aligning IT services with business objectives. Through these relationships, IT service managers can ensure that their services meet the needs of the business, remain aligned with its strategic direction, and are valued by its members. While building these relationships requires effort and skill, the payoff in terms of service effectiveness, business alignment, and IT value is well worth it.

10.3 Customer Satisfaction and Service Experience Management

Customer satisfaction and service experience management are pivotal aspects of IT Service Management. As the world becomes increasingly digital, the quality of IT services directly influences the overall experience customers have with a company. Therefore, a comprehensive understanding and effective management of customer satisfaction and service experience is crucial. In this section, we will delve into the importance of customer satisfaction, the concept of service experience management, and strategies for enhancing both in the context of IT services.

Understanding customer satisfaction begins with acknowledging its importance. In essence, customer satisfaction reflects the degree to which a product or service meets or surpasses customer expectations. In the context of IT services, these customers may be internal users within the organization or external clients who interact with the company's IT systems and services.

A high level of customer satisfaction leads to a multitude of benefits. It fosters customer loyalty, promotes positive word-of-mouth, and can differentiate an organization in a crowded marketplace. From an internal perspective, satisfied customers (users) are more likely to adopt new systems, follow processes, and be forgiving when issues arise.

Service experience management broadens the perspective beyond individual transactions or interactions. It is a holistic approach that considers the entire customer journey with the IT service - from initial contact, through usage, to post-service interactions. This journey may involve multiple touchpoints (like service desk, self-service portal, and email notifications), and each of these touchpoints contributes to the overall service experience.

A positive service experience leads to enhanced customer satisfaction. It also provides an opportunity for the organization to exceed customer expectations by creating pleasant surprises and 'wow' moments. This is increasingly important as customers today, accustomed to consumer-grade technology experiences, expect the same level of smooth, seamless, and pleasant interactions with corporate IT services.

The following strategies can be employed to enhance customer satisfaction and service experience:

i. **Customer Centricity:** Place customers at the heart of service design and delivery. Understand their needs, expectations, and pain points. Use this understanding to design services that meet their needs and deliver them in a way that matches their preferences.

ii. **Service Quality Management:** Invest in improving the quality of IT services. This includes the technical aspects (like availability, reliability, and performance) and the service aspects (like responsiveness, empathy, and communication).

iii. **Customer Feedback:** Regularly collect and analyze customer feedback. This can be achieved through various methods such as surveys, interviews, or focus groups. Use this feedback to identify areas of improvement and monitor progress over time.

iv. **Service Experience Design:** Design the service experience intentionally and holistically. Map out the customer journey, identify touchpoints, and design each touchpoint to contribute positively to the overall experience. This includes not just the major touchpoints but also the minor ones that can make a difference.

v. **Service Recovery:** Despite best efforts, things will go wrong. When they do, effective service recovery can turn a negative experience into a positive one. This involves acknowledging the issue, apologizing sincerely, fixing the problem promptly, and compensating if necessary.

vi. **Continual Improvement:** Make continual improvement a part of the culture. Always look for opportunities to improve customer satisfaction and service experience, implement improvements, and measure their impact.

In conclusion, customer satisfaction and service experience management are critical aspects of IT Service Management. They contribute significantly to the success of the organization and its IT services. By understanding their importance, adopting a holistic perspective, and employing effective strategies, organizations can enhance customer satisfaction and create memorable service experiences.

10.4 Business-IT Alignment and Value Creation

Business-IT alignment and value creation form the crux of the strategic role that IT services play in today's digital-driven business environment. The notion of IT merely acting as a supporting function has significantly evolved; it is now considered a strategic partner capable of driving business growth and innovation. This shift in perception is central to the concept of business-IT alignment and the resulting value creation. In this section, we will explore what business-IT alignment entails, its importance, the concept of IT value creation, and strategies for achieving alignment and demonstrating value.

Business-IT alignment refers to the synchronization of business strategies and IT strategies, ensuring that the technology supports business objectives and adds value. It's not just about having technology in place but also about ensuring that the technology serves a meaningful purpose, helping the organization achieve its goals.

Aligning IT with the business is not a one-off task but a dynamic process that needs constant attention as both business objectives and technologies evolve. The importance of this alignment cannot be overstated. It can lead to more effective decision-making, optimal resource allocation, better return on IT investments, improved competitive positioning, and, ultimately, enhanced business performance.

IT value creation, on the other hand, is about the IT function's contribution to business success. It involves demonstrating how IT services and initiatives contribute to achieving business objectives, enhancing operational efficiency, and driving innovation. It goes beyond just maintaining operational stability and extends to enabling business growth and transformation.

The following strategies can be employed to enhance business-IT alignment and value creation:

i. **Understanding Business Objectives:** This is the starting point for any alignment effort. IT leaders must have a clear understanding of the organization's strategic goals and how these goals translate into tactical objectives. This understanding helps in prioritizing IT initiatives that directly support these objectives.

ii. **Involvement in Strategic Planning:** IT leadership should be involved in business strategic planning from the outset. This allows them to provide insights on how technology can be leveraged to achieve business goals and ensures that IT strategy is developed with a clear understanding of business direction.

iii. **Strong Business Relationship Management:** Regular interaction with business stakeholders aids in understanding their needs, expectations, and pain points. This understanding is crucial in aligning IT services with business needs and demonstrating the value that IT provides.

iv. **Effective Communication:** Communicating the value of IT in business terms is critical. IT leaders need to effectively communicate the benefits of IT initiatives, the value they add, and how they support the business strategy.

v. **Measurement and Reporting:** Establishing key performance indicators (KPIs) aligned with business objectives helps quantify the value that IT services provide.

Regular reporting on these KPIs further cements the value proposition of IT.

vi. **Promoting IT Innovation:** Encouraging and fostering a culture of innovation within the IT function can lead to novel solutions that offer a competitive advantage and create business value.

vii. **Continual Improvement:** Continually striving for improved IT services and processes ensures the IT function remains relevant and valuable in a rapidly evolving business environment.

In conclusion, the alignment of business and IT strategies is essential in the contemporary business world. IT is no longer a siloed function; it's a strategic partner that enables business success. By focusing on business-IT alignment and IT value creation, organizations can optimize their IT investments, enhance decision-making, and achieve their business objectives more effectively.

Chapter 11: Auditing, Compliance, and Certification

Chapter 11 delves into the fundamental aspects of auditing, compliance, and certification as they pertain to IT Service Management and ISO/IEC 20000-1. These concepts are crucial for validating the effectiveness of the Service Management System (SMS) implemented by an organization, ensuring adherence to the specified standards, and instilling confidence among stakeholders regarding the organization's service delivery capabilities.

This chapter aims to demystify the process of conducting internal and external audits, managing compliance with ISO/IEC 20000-1, and achieving certification. It will guide readers on how to prepare for audits, understand the audit process, and use audit findings to drive continual improvement in service management practices.

Furthermore, it will highlight the importance of maintaining ongoing compliance with ISO/IEC 20000-1, even after achieving certification, to ensure that service management practices remain current, relevant, and effective over time.

By the end of this chapter, readers will appreciate the role of auditing, compliance, and certification in enhancing their IT service management practices, promoting transparency and accountability, and building a robust, effective, and standards-compliant Service Management System.

11.1 Internal Audits and Self-Assessment

An internal audit and self-assessment are essential components in the successful implementation and ongoing management of ISO/IEC 20000-1 service management systems (SMS). The primary purpose of these processes is to evaluate the effectiveness of an organization's SMS and to identify areas for improvement.

In conducting an internal audit, organizations can delve deep into their service management processes to identify any discrepancies or inconsistencies with the ISO/IEC 20000-1 standard. This introspection facilitates an understanding of the organization's position in terms of compliance and provides a platform for improving processes and procedures.

Self-assessment, on the other hand, enables organizations to periodically examine their service management practices to ensure ongoing compliance with the ISO/IEC 20000-1 standard. It is a tool for organizations to review their performance, assess their strengths and weaknesses, and devise strategies for improvement.

When beginning an internal audit, the organization must first establish an audit scope. The audit scope identifies the parts of the organization and the processes that will be audited. This could be department-specific or span the whole organization, depending on the organization's size and structure.

Following this, an audit plan is developed which outlines the audit's objectives, the areas to be audited, the audit schedule, and the resources required for the audit. The audit plan also determines the audit criteria, which is essentially the set of policies, procedures, and requirements against which the organization's service management practices will be evaluated.

The audit process involves collecting and analyzing evidence through various methods such as interviews, observation of processes, and review of documentation. The auditors evaluate this evidence to determine if the organization's service management practices conform to the audit criteria.

At the end of the audit, an audit report is produced which outlines the audit findings, including areas of non-compliance and opportunities for improvement. This report is then presented to the management of the organization for review and action.

The self-assessment process, much like the internal audit, involves a review of the organization's service management practices. However, instead of being conducted by independent auditors, self-assessments are often conducted by the organization's personnel. This allows for a more detailed and nuanced understanding of the organization's service management practices and facilitates a sense of ownership and engagement in the improvement process.

One of the key benefits of conducting self-assessments is that it encourages a culture of continual improvement within the organization. By regularly reviewing and assessing their service management practices, organizations can ensure that they are continually improving and refining their processes to deliver high-quality services.

Another advantage of self-assessments is that they can help prepare the organization for external audits. By regularly conducting self-assessments, organizations can identify and address any areas of non-compliance before the external audit, thereby improving their chances of achieving ISO/IEC 20000-1 certification.

In conclusion, internal audits and self-assessments are critical tools for ensuring compliance with ISO/IEC 20000-1. They provide an opportunity for organizations to reflect on their service management practices, identify areas for improvement, and ensure that they are delivering the highest quality services to their customers. Whether an organization is seeking ISO/IEC 20000-1 certification or simply aiming to improve its service management practices, internal audits, and self-assessments can provide valuable insights and direction for improvement.

11.2 Preparing for External Audits

An external audit is a formal, independent evaluation of an organization's service management system (SMS) in line with the ISO/IEC 20000-1 standard. Unlike an internal audit or self-assessment, which is usually conducted by personnel within the organization, an external audit is carried out by an impartial third-party auditor. The ultimate goal of the external audit is to obtain ISO/IEC 20000-1 certification, demonstrating the organization's commitment to delivering quality IT services that meet international standards.

The process of preparing for an external audit requires careful planning and commitment from all levels of the organization. This preparation process often involves a multi-pronged approach, which includes understanding the standard, conducting internal audits, rectifying non-compliance issues, training personnel, and liaising with the external auditor.

Understanding the ISO/IEC 20000-1 standard is the first step in preparing for an external audit. The organization needs to thoroughly understand the requirements of the standard, including the specifics of what the auditor will be looking for during the audit. Each clause of the standard should be reviewed in detail, and the expectations fully comprehended. Many organizations find it useful to hold workshops or training sessions to ensure that everyone involved understands the requirements of the standard.

Next, conducting internal audits and self-assessments is crucial in the preparatory stage. These exercises provide a snapshot of the current state of the organization's service management processes, helping identify areas that comply with the standard and those that require improvement. The organization can then devise an action plan to address any non-compliance issues identified during these audits.

Remedying non-compliance issues is a crucial aspect of the preparation. It involves the implementation of the action plan devised after the internal audits. This stage may include the development of new processes, modification of existing ones, training of staff, or any other measures necessary to ensure compliance with the standard. It is crucial to monitor and document these changes as they can form part of the evidence required during the external audit.

Training of personnel forms an integral part of the preparation. Training helps ensure that all staff members understand their roles and responsibilities concerning the standard. It also ensures that they are well-prepared to answer any questions that the auditor may have during the audit.

Finally, liaising with the external auditor is an important part of the preparation process. This includes establishing the audit's scope, discussing the audit plan, and agreeing on a suitable date for the audit. In addition, the organization should clarify any doubts or concerns they may have about the audit process with the auditor. This helps ensure a smooth audit process.

As the audit day approaches, the organization needs to ensure that all necessary documentation is readily available for the auditor. This includes documentation on the organization's service management processes, records of internal audits, evidence of corrective actions, and any other documents the auditor may require.

During the external audit, the organization should aim to be transparent and cooperative with the auditor. It's essential to remember that the auditor is not an adversary but a partner aiming to help the organization improve its service management practices.

Post-audit, the organization should carefully review the auditor's report and take action on the findings. If the audit is successful and the organization meets the requirements of the standard, it will receive the ISO/IEC 20000-1 certification. However, if non-compliances are identified, the organization must take corrective actions and may need to undergo a re-audit to achieve certification.

In conclusion, preparing for an external audit requires a structured and meticulous approach. Understanding the ISO/IEC 20000-1 standard, conducting internal audits, rectifying non-compliance issues, training personnel, and liaising with the external auditor are all essential elements of this preparation. Through thorough preparation, organizations can not only achieve ISO/IEC 20000-1 certification but also significantly improve their service management practices.

11.3 Achieving ISO/IEC 20000-1 Certification

Achieving ISO/IEC 20000-1 certification is a significant milestone for any organization seeking to demonstrate its commitment to delivering high-quality IT services. The certification provides assurance to stakeholders, clients, and partners that the organization adheres to internationally recognized service management standards. However, obtaining the certification is not a simple task; it demands careful planning, resource allocation, and sustained efforts. Here is a detailed guide on the journey to achieving ISO/IEC 20000-1 certification.

Step 1: Initial Assessment and Gap Analysis

Before embarking on the certification journey, it's important to assess where your organization currently stands concerning ISO/IEC 20000-1 requirements. Conduct a gap analysis to identify areas where your service management system (SMS) is already compliant and where improvements are needed. This will give you a clear picture of the amount of work required to meet the standard's requirements.

Step 2: Obtain Management Commitment

Management commitment is crucial to the successful implementation of ISO/IEC 20000-1. Secure support from top management by illustrating the benefits of certification, such as improved service quality, reduced costs, and enhanced customer satisfaction. This support is essential in ensuring that sufficient resources and priority are allocated to the certification project.

Step 3: Develop an Implementation Plan

Once you've obtained management commitment, develop a detailed implementation plan. This should include setting objectives, defining roles and responsibilities, allocating resources, and setting a realistic timeline for the implementation. Ensure that the plan is communicated throughout the organization and that all staff understand their roles in achieving certification.

Step 4: Train and Educate Staff

Education and training are essential components of the certification process. Ensure that your staff is aware of the importance of ISO/IEC 20000-1 and that they understand the specific requirements of the standard. Offer training programs to equip staff with the knowledge and skills necessary to contribute to the successful implementation of the SMS.

Step 5: Develop and Implement Processes

In accordance with the requirements of ISO/IEC 20000-1, develop and implement the processes necessary for an effective SMS. This may involve the development of new processes, or the modification of existing ones, to ensure they are aligned with the standard. Document these processes clearly and ensure that they are communicated and understood throughout the organization.

Step 6: Monitor and Measure

Once the SMS has been implemented, it is essential to monitor and measure its performance against the objectives you have set. Develop key performance indicators (KPIs) that are aligned with your objectives, and use them to monitor the effectiveness of your SMS. Use this data to make continual improvements to your service management processes.

Step 7: Internal Audit
Conduct an internal audit to verify that your SMS is compliant with the requirements of ISO/IEC 20000-1. This will help to identify any remaining non-compliance issues that need to be addressed before the external audit. The internal audit should be carried out by individuals who are independent of the area being audited to ensure objectivity.

Step 8: Management Review
Following the internal audit, a management review should be conducted. This is a formal review by top management, focusing on the suitability, adequacy, and effectiveness of the SMS. The management review should take into account any non-conformities identified in the internal audit and make decisions on improvements.

Step 9: External Audit
Upon completion of the internal audit and management review, and once you believe that your organization is compliant with the standard, it is time to undergo the external audit. This involves a third-party certification body auditing your SMS to verify that it complies with the requirements of ISO/IEC 20000-1. Be transparent and cooperative during this audit, providing the auditors with all the necessary evidence of compliance.

Step 10: Certification and Continual Improvement
If your SMS meets the requirements of the standard, your organization will be awarded ISO/IEC 20000-1 certification. However, certification is not the end of the journey. You should maintain a culture of continual improvement, regularly reviewing and improving

your service management processes to ensure ongoing compliance and improved performance.

In conclusion, achieving ISO/IEC 20000-1 certification requires a systematic and committed approach. The journey may be challenging, but the benefits reaped, including improved service delivery, customer satisfaction, and business efficiency, make it a worthwhile endeavor.

11.4 Sustaining Compliance and Continual Improvement

Achieving ISO/IEC 20000-1 certification is a significant accomplishment that attests to the organization's commitment to adhering to international service management standards. However, the journey does not end with certification; organizations must strive to sustain compliance and foster a culture of continual improvement. This chapter delves into strategies to maintain compliance with the standard and ways to ensure that the service management system (SMS) continuously evolves and improves.

Sustaining Compliance

Maintaining compliance with ISO/IEC 20000-1 necessitates ongoing diligence and vigilance. Complacency after certification can lead to slipping standards, resulting in decreased quality of services and potentially losing the certification.

Regular Audits: Internal audits should be conducted at regular intervals to ensure continued adherence to the standard's requirements. These audits help identify non-conformities and areas for improvement. The outcomes of these audits must be taken seriously, with prompt action taken to address identified gaps.

Management Reviews: Senior management must periodically review the SMS to ensure its continued suitability, adequacy, and effectiveness. These reviews should consider changes in the organization, such as strategic direction or resources and the need for changes to the SMS. The focus should be on improving customer satisfaction and service delivery.

Employee Training: Sustaining compliance requires that all employees understand the importance of the SMS and their role in maintaining it. Regular training and refreshers are crucial to ensure staff stay updated about the service management processes and their roles in upholding the standards.

Continual Improvement

Continual improvement is a key principle of ISO/IEC 20000-1. It's about not just maintaining compliance but also about finding ways to perform better, improving service delivery and customer satisfaction.

Process Improvement: Continually evaluate and refine the service management processes. The use of key performance indicators (KPIs) can help measure process performance and identify areas that require improvement. Techniques like Lean Six Sigma can be valuable in identifying and eliminating waste, reducing variability, and improving process efficiency.

Technology Adaptation: Technology is a vital enabler of service management. Stay abreast of technological advancements that can make service delivery more efficient and effective. This could involve the adoption of new service management tools, automation of manual tasks, or the use of data analytics for informed decision-making.

Customer Feedback: Customer feedback is a goldmine for improvement. Regularly gather and analyze customer feedback to understand their needs and expectations better. Act on this feedback to improve services and enhance customer satisfaction.

Continual Improvement Culture: Encourage a culture that values improvement. Employees should feel empowered to suggest improvements and changes. Rewarding improvement initiatives can also go a long way in fostering a proactive improvement culture.

In conclusion, sustaining compliance with ISO/IEC 20000-1 and fostering continual improvement is an ongoing endeavor. It requires commitment at all levels of the organization, regular review and improvement of the SMS, and an organizational culture that values excellence and improvement. In this journey, the organization not only maintains its ISO/IEC 20000-1 certification but also delivers superior services that meet customer needs and expectations, contributing to its overall success.

Chapter 12: Emerging Trends and Future of IT Service Management

Chapter 12 delves into the future of IT service management, examining the trends shaping its evolution and the potential challenges and opportunities these present. From the rise of automation and AI to the increasing emphasis on customer experience and service integration, this chapter provides a glimpse into the rapidly changing landscape of ITSM. Understanding these trends is crucial for any organization aiming to stay competitive, continually improve its service delivery, and ultimately provide value to its customers and stakeholders. Armed with this knowledge, ITSM professionals can better navigate the future, aligning their strategies with emerging trends and leveraging them to deliver efficient, effective, and customer-centric services.

12.1 The Impact of Digital Transformation on ITSM

The impact of digital transformation on IT Service Management (ITSM) has been profound and continues to redefine the landscape of service delivery in organizations. This paradigm shift is not just about the adoption of new technologies but also requires a change in mindset, culture, and the way we do business. Let's explore how digital transformation impacts ITSM.

Firstly, the very concept of service delivery has evolved with digital transformation. Earlier, the IT department was seen as a back-office function that supports the business. However, in the digital age, IT has moved to the front and center, playing a strategic role in business innovation, growth, and customer engagement. Services are no longer just about supporting business functions; they are about creating value for the business and its customers. ITSM practices have therefore evolved to support this strategic role, focusing more on service value, customer experience, and business outcomes rather than just operational efficiency.

Moreover, digital transformation has brought about a shift in the way services are designed and managed. With the adoption of cloud technologies, services are now more scalable, flexible, and adaptable to changing business needs. This has led to a change in the ITSM processes, with more emphasis on service strategy and design and less on operational aspects like incident and problem management. ITSM has also had to incorporate new practices like DevOps and Agile, which focus on speed, collaboration, and continuous improvement.

In addition, the tools used for service management have also evolved with digital transformation. Automation and artificial intelligence (AI) have become key enablers of efficient and effective service delivery. AI can be used for tasks like incident prediction, problem diagnosis, and service request fulfillment, reducing manual effort and improving the speed and accuracy of these processes. Automation can be used to streamline and standardize processes, reducing the risk of errors and improving efficiency. These technologies have led to the emergence of new roles in ITSM, like service automation engineer and AIops specialist, and require new skills and competencies.

Digital transformation has also brought about changes in the way ITSM is governed and measured. With the increased complexity and pace of change, traditional governance models and metrics may no longer be sufficient. Governance now needs to be more flexible and adaptive, able to respond to changes quickly and effectively. Metrics need to focus more on customer experience and business value rather than just operational efficiency. This has led to the adoption of concepts like Lean IT and value stream mapping in ITSM, which focus on eliminating waste and maximizing value.

Furthermore, digital transformation has also increased the importance of security and risk management in ITSM. With the increasing use of digital technologies, organizations are more exposed to cyber threats and need to manage the associated risks. ITSM practices have therefore evolved to incorporate security considerations into the service lifecycle, from design and transition to operation and improvement. This has led to the emergence of new practices like SecOps, which integrate security into IT operations.

In conclusion, the impact of digital transformation on ITSM is significant and pervasive, touching every aspect of service delivery. It requires a shift in mindset, practices, tools, and skills. However, it also presents an opportunity for ITSM to evolve and become a strategic enabler of business value rather than just a support function. By understanding these impacts and responding to them effectively, organizations can leverage ITSM to navigate the digital transformation journey successfully. The future of ITSM is exciting, and the opportunities are endless for those who are prepared to embrace the change.

12.2 Agile and DevOps in Service Management

Agile and DevOps have made a significant impact on IT Service Management (ITSM), driving it to evolve and adapt to the changing business landscape. The traditional approach to ITSM, which is process-heavy and often slow to respond to changes, does not align well with the speed and flexibility required in today's digital age. As organizations strive for greater agility and efficiency, Agile and DevOps methodologies have found their way into service management practices, creating a transformative shift in how services are designed, delivered, and managed.

Agile ITSM reflects the adoption of Agile principles and practices in service management, focusing on people and interactions over processes and tools, customer collaboration over contract negotiation, and responding to change over following a rigid plan. Agile emphasizes iterative development, regular feedback, and constant improvement, allowing organizations to adapt quickly to changing customer needs and market conditions.

In the ITSM context, Agile can lead to more responsive and customer-focused services. For instance, service desk teams could use an Agile approach to manage incidents and requests, prioritizing work based on customer impact and business value and addressing them in short, focused iterations (or sprints). Regular reviews and retrospectives can help to identify improvements and adjust plans as needed.

Furthermore, Agile can also improve the service design and transition processes. Instead of designing and implementing services in a linear, waterfall manner, teams can adopt an iterative approach, delivering small increments of service and obtaining feedback from customers before proceeding further. This can reduce the risk of failure, improve customer satisfaction, and speed up the delivery of services.

Meanwhile, DevOps - a portmanteau of "development" and "operations" - is a culture, movement, or practice that emphasizes the collaboration and communication of both software developers and other IT professionals while automating the process of software delivery and infrastructure changes. It aims at establishing a culture and environment where building, testing, and releasing software can happen rapidly, frequently, and more reliably.

In the context of ITSM, DevOps promotes a shift from siloed to integrated operations. Dev and Ops teams work together across the entire service lifecycle, from design through the development process to production support. This approach helps to break down barriers, improve communication, and foster a culture of shared responsibility for service quality and performance.

DevOps also brings a strong focus on automation to ITSM, leveraging tools and technologies to automate routine tasks such as testing, deployment, and configuration management. This can significantly reduce manual effort, improve efficiency, and reduce the risk of errors. Incident, problem, and change management can all benefit from

DevOps practices like continuous integration and continuous delivery (CI/CD), infrastructure as code (IaC), and automated monitoring and alerting.

Moreover, DevOps introduces practices like continuous improvement and learning into ITSM. Post-incident reviews, and blameless postmortems become a part of the process, helping teams to learn from failures and prevent a recurrence. This focus on learning and improvement aligns well with the ITSM principle of continual service improvement.

The integration of Agile and DevOps into ITSM is not without challenges. It requires a cultural shift, as well as changes to practices, roles, and tools. Organizations need to invest in training and development to build the necessary skills and also consider changes to governance and metrics to align with the Agile and DevOps ways of working.

However, the benefits of Agile and DevOps in service management are substantial. They can lead to more responsive, efficient, and customer-focused services, faster delivery, improved quality, and higher levels of innovation. By embracing these methodologies, organizations can ensure their ITSM practices are fit for the digital age and capable of delivering maximum value to the business.

12.3 Cloud Computing and IT Service Delivery

Cloud computing has emerged as a transformative technology, reshaping IT Service Delivery in unprecedented ways. As organizations increasingly move their operations to the cloud to enhance efficiency, scalability, and agility, IT Service Management (ITSM) finds itself at a crossroads, having to accommodate and adapt to this significant shift.

The cloud computing model provides on-demand network access to a shared pool of configurable computing resources. These resources can be rapidly provisioned and released with minimal management effort or service provider interaction, leading to major changes in IT service delivery and management. There are three primary cloud service models: Infrastructure as a Service (IaaS), Platform as a Service (PaaS), and Software as a Service (SaaS).

Firstly, the cloud has greatly accelerated service delivery. Traditional IT service delivery requires substantial time and resources for procurement, installation, and configuration of infrastructure. With the cloud, IT services can now be delivered in minutes rather than weeks or months. This enhanced speed and agility can give businesses a significant competitive advantage, enabling them to respond faster to changing market conditions and customer demands.

Furthermore, cloud computing introduces a new level of scalability to IT service delivery. In a traditional IT environment, organizations needed to plan for peak demand, often resulting in underutilized resources during off-peak periods. In contrast, cloud services can be dynamically scaled up or down to match demand, resulting in more efficient use of resources and cost savings. This elasticity is particularly beneficial for businesses with fluctuating or unpredictable workloads.

The cloud also brings significant changes to the financial model of IT service delivery. Traditional IT requires significant capital expenditure (CapEx) for hardware, software, and infrastructure. In contrast, cloud services typically follow an operational expenditure (OpEx) model, where costs are based on usage. This shift from CapEx to OpEx can provide businesses with more flexibility and control over IT spending.

Despite its many benefits, the shift to the cloud also brings challenges to ITSM. One of the major challenges is the management of multi-cloud and hybrid cloud environments. As organizations often use services from multiple cloud providers or maintain some resources on-premises, managing these complex environments can be challenging. ITSM processes and tools need to evolve to provide seamless management across these diverse environments.

Another significant challenge is cloud security and compliance. As data and services move to the cloud, they are subject to new risks and vulnerabilities. ITSM needs to incorporate new processes and controls to manage these risks and ensure compliance with data protection and privacy regulations.

Moreover, the shift to the cloud requires a change in skills and competencies. Traditional IT skills may not be sufficient for managing cloud services. Organizations need to invest in cloud-related training and development to ensure their IT teams have the necessary skills for cloud management, including knowledge of cloud platforms, automation and orchestration tools, cloud security, and cloud governance.

In the cloud era, ITSM must evolve from a technology-centric to a service-centric approach. IT teams need to understand and align with business requirements, manage relationships with multiple cloud service providers, and ensure the delivery of high-quality, reliable services to end users. ITSM processes like service catalog management, service level management, and service portfolio management become increasingly important in this context.

Despite these challenges, the move to the cloud is an opportunity for ITSM to become more strategic and valuable to the business. By leveraging the power of the cloud, ITSM can drive digital transformation, enhance agility, and deliver more value to the business. This requires ITSM to not just adapt to the cloud but to embrace it fully, viewing it as an enabler of innovation and a driver of business growth.

12.4 Artificial Intelligence and Automation in ITSM

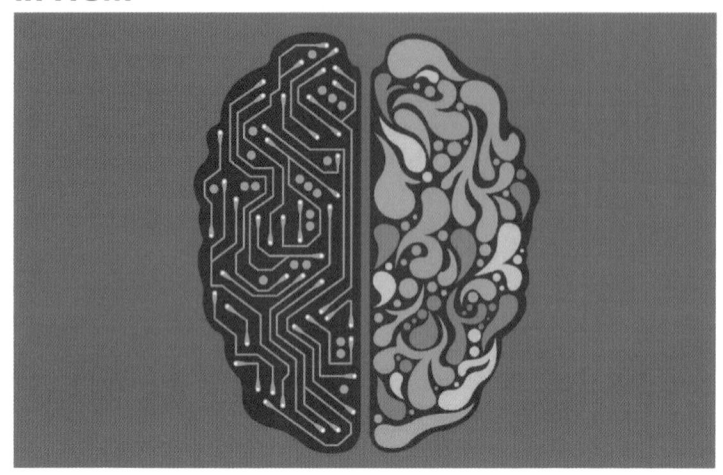

The integration of Artificial Intelligence (AI) and automation into IT Service Management (ITSM) has the potential to revolutionize the way organizations deliver IT services. These technologies can enhance efficiency, improve service quality, and provide innovative capabilities that were once beyond reach. However, the shift towards AI and automation also brings with it new challenges and implications that need to be addressed.

Artificial Intelligence, with its subset Machine Learning (ML), leverages computational algorithms to analyze large amounts of data, identify patterns, make predictions, and automate decision-making. Automation, on the other hand, is the use of technology to perform tasks with minimal human intervention.

AI and automation have a profound impact on several aspects of ITSM. For instance, AI-powered chatbots and virtual assistants are increasingly used for IT service desk operations. They can handle routine inquiries, guide users through problem-solving steps, and even automate some tasks, thereby freeing up service desk agents to handle more complex issues. This not only increases efficiency but also improves user satisfaction by providing immediate responses and 24/7 availability.

Predictive analytics is another area where AI has significant potential. Machine learning algorithms can analyze large volumes of IT service data to predict potential failures or disruptions. This allows IT teams to proactively address issues before they impact service levels. Similarly, AI can enhance the accuracy of IT capacity forecasting, leading to more efficient resource allocation and cost management.

Automation plays a critical role in various ITSM processes. In Incident Management, automation can speed up incident detection, logging, and categorization. Automated workflows can ensure that incidents are routed to the appropriate teams promptly, reducing resolution times. In Change Management, automation can streamline the change approval process and automatically deploy approved changes, reducing the risk of errors and downtime.

Automation also has a significant impact on Configuration Management. Automated discovery tools can continuously scan the IT environment to identify configuration items and their relationships, ensuring that the Configuration Management Database (CMDB) is always up-to-date. This not only reduces the time and effort required for configuration management but also improves the accuracy of information used for impact analysis and root cause analysis.

AI and automation also facilitate the implementation of self-healing systems. These systems leverage AI to detect problems, diagnose root causes, and initiate corrective actions without human intervention. This can dramatically reduce downtime and improve service availability.

However, the shift towards AI and automation in ITSM is not without challenges. One of the key challenges is the potential impact on jobs and roles. While AI and automation can reduce the need for routine tasks, they require new skills and competencies for implementation, management, and oversight. This requires a focus on reskilling and upskilling IT staff to enable them to work effectively with these new technologies.

Another challenge is data quality. AI algorithms depend on large volumes of high-quality data to function effectively. Inaccurate or incomplete data can lead to erroneous predictions or decisions. Therefore, organizations must ensure robust data governance and quality control mechanisms.

Additionally, the use of AI and automation raises ethical and privacy concerns. Organizations need to consider how they use and protect data, how they ensure transparency in AI decision-making, and how they prevent bias in AI algorithms.

Despite these challenges, the potential benefits of AI and automation in ITSM are immense. They provide an opportunity for ITSM to enhance efficiency, improve service quality, and drive innovation. However, the successful integration of these technologies requires a strategic approach, focusing on aligning technology with business needs, managing organizational and cultural change, and addressing the ethical and privacy implications.

Appendix

ISO/IEC 20000-1:2018 Standard at a Glance

The ISO/IEC 20000-1:2018 is a globally recognized standard that sets the criteria for effective IT Service Management (ITSM). Developed by the International Organization for Standardization (ISO) and the International Electrotechnical Commission (IEC), the standard defines the requirements for the service management system (SMS) necessary to deliver managed services of acceptable quality for customers, whether they are internal or external.

The ISO/IEC 20000-1:2018 replaces the earlier version ISO/IEC 20000-1:2011 and features several important updates. One of the most critical updates is the adoption of the high-level structure (HLS) of ISO, also used by other management systems standards like ISO 9001 and ISO 14001. This facilitates the integration of various management systems within an organization.

The structure of the ISO/IEC 20000-1:2018 includes the following main clauses: Scope, Normative References, Terms and Definitions, Context of the Organization, Leadership, Planning, Support, Operation, Performance Evaluation, and Improvement. Each of these sections presents specific requirements that an organization must fulfill to comply with the standard.

The 'Scope' clause outlines the applications of the standard, while 'Normative References' provides reference documents that are indispensable for the application of this document. 'Terms and Definitions' gives a detailed explanation of key terms used in the standard.

'Context of the Organization' is a new addition to the 2018 version and emphasizes the understanding of the organization and its context, as well as the needs and expectations of interested parties. This clause underscores the significance of aligning the SMS with the business strategy and understanding how external and internal factors can impact the SMS.

The 'Leadership' clause focuses on the role of top management in establishing a customer-focused service management policy, defining roles, responsibilities, and authorities in the SMS, and promoting a service management culture within the organization.

The 'Planning' section specifies requirements for addressing risks and opportunities, setting service management objectives, and planning changes to the SMS. The 'Support' clause covers resource management, competence, awareness, communication, and documented information.

The 'Operation' clause is central to the standard, encompassing the planning, design, transition, delivery, and improvement of services. It includes specific processes like incident management, request management, problem management, and release and deployment management.

'Performance Evaluation' mandates the monitoring, measurement, analysis, and evaluation of SMS and services. This includes internal audits and management reviews to ensure the SMS is effective and aligned with the organization's strategic objectives.

The 'Improvement' section emphasizes the need for continual improvement of the SMS and services. It includes requirements for identifying and rectifying non-conformities, analyzing root causes, and taking corrective actions.

It is important to note that while ISO/IEC 20000-1:2018 provides a robust framework for ITSM, it is flexible enough to be adapted to the needs of different organizations, regardless of their size, type, or nature of the services provided. Compliance with the standard demonstrates an organization's commitment to quality service delivery and continual improvement. This not only improves customer satisfaction but also enhances the organization's credibility and competitive edge.

However, achieving ISO/IEC 20000-1:2018 certification requires considerable effort. It involves establishing and documenting the SMS, implementing the required processes, conducting internal audits, and undergoing an external audit by an accredited certification body. Furthermore, maintaining the certification requires ongoing effort to ensure continual improvement and compliance with the evolving standard.

In conclusion, ISO/IEC 20000-1:2018 provides a comprehensive and adaptable framework for effective ITSM. It emphasizes the alignment of IT services with business objectives, a consistent and structured approach to service delivery, and a culture of continual improvement. While the journey to certification can be challenging, the benefits in terms of improved service quality, customer satisfaction, and business efficiency make it a worthwhile endeavor.

Sample Templates and Checklists for ISO/IEC 20000-1 Implementation

The successful implementation of ISO/IEC 20000-1 requires a structured and organized approach, and the use of templates and checklists can greatly aid this process. They provide a clear and simplified way of ensuring that all requirements of the standard have been considered and addressed.

Here, we will go through some examples of the types of templates and checklists that can be used at different stages of the ISO/IEC 20000-1 implementation process. However, remember that these templates and checklists should be adapted to fit the specific context and requirements of your organization.

   i. **ISO/IEC 20000-1 Readiness Checklist:** This checklist is used at the beginning of the implementation process to evaluate the current state of the organization's service management system (SMS). It covers the major clauses of the ISO/IEC 20000-1 standard, helping the organization identify gaps in the existing system and determine what needs to be done to achieve compliance.

ii. **Risk Management Template:** One of the key requirements of ISO/IEC 20000-1 is the identification and management of risks and opportunities. A risk management template can help in listing all potential risks, their likelihood, potential impact, and planned mitigation strategies. This not only aids in risk assessment but also in documenting the process for audit purposes.

iii. **Service Management Plan Template:** This template serves as a guide in developing a comprehensive service management plan. It includes sections for defining service objectives, setting up service delivery and management processes, defining roles and responsibilities, and establishing performance metrics and targets.

iv. **Service Level Agreement (SLA) Template:** An SLA is a crucial document in ITSM as it outlines the agreed service quality targets between the service provider and the customer. The template includes details such as the scope of the service, performance metrics, responsibilities of both parties and penalties for non-compliance.

v. **Process Documentation Template:** Each service management process should be clearly defined and documented. The process documentation template includes sections describing the purpose of the process, the process activities, roles and responsibilities, process inputs and outputs, and process performance metrics.

vi. **Internal Audit Checklist:** An internal audit is a mandatory part of ISO/IEC 20000-1 compliance, and a checklist simplifies the audit process. The checklist contains a list of all the standard requirements, and auditors can use it to check whether the organization meets each requirement. It can also be used to record evidence and findings.

vii. **Management Review Meeting Agenda Template:** Regular management reviews are essential for the continual improvement of the SMS. The agenda template outlines the topics to be covered during the review meeting, including the status of previous actions, feedback from interested parties, performance metrics, audit results, and improvement opportunities.

viii. **Non-Conformance Report Template:** This template is used to document any non-conformances identified during audits or other assessments. It includes information about the non-conformance, its impact, root cause, corrective action taken, and follow-up actions.

ix. **Continual Improvement Register:** This template helps track all improvement initiatives within the organization. It includes details such as the description of the improvement, the person responsible, status, and expected outcomes.

These are just some examples of templates and checklists that can be used during ISO/IEC 20000-1 implementation. They can be developed internally or sourced from professional bodies or consulting firms. The key is to ensure that they are used consistently and effectively to support the implementation and maintenance of the SMS.

Remember, achieving ISO/IEC 20000-1 certification is not a one-time event but a commitment to ongoing service quality and improvement. These tools will provide a solid foundation for your organization's journey toward ITSM excellence.

Case Studies and Success Stories

Case studies and success stories serve as essential tools in understanding the practical application and benefits of the ISO/IEC 20000-1 standard. They offer insights into how different organizations have successfully implemented the standard, the challenges they faced, and how they overcame them. In this chapter, we will explore two detailed case studies from diverse industries.

Case Study 1: A Large Financial Institution

A large financial institution, with operations in over 50 countries decided to implement ISO/IEC 20000-1 to enhance its IT service management (ITSM) practices. The organization's goal was to increase the efficiency and effectiveness of its IT services and improve customer satisfaction.

The implementation began with a gap analysis to assess the current state of the institution's service management system. The findings revealed a lack of standardized processes across different departments, which led to inconsistencies in service delivery and management.

The institution then established a project team consisting of IT professionals from various departments. They began by drafting a service management policy that aligned with the organization's strategic goals. The team also developed detailed service management plans for each department, clearly defining roles, responsibilities, and procedures.

One of the main challenges was resistance to change among employees. To address this, the project team organized training sessions and workshops to highlight the benefits of ISO/IEC 20000-1 and its relevance to their roles. The training also covered the new processes and how to apply them.

After a year of diligent efforts, the financial institution achieved ISO/IEC 20000-1 certification. This milestone resulted in significant improvements in service delivery times, reduced incidents, and increased customer satisfaction. It also brought about a cultural shift within the organization, with employees now viewing service management from a more strategic perspective.

Case Study 2: A Global Software Company

A leading software company with customers around the globe decided to pursue ISO/IEC 20000-1 certification to enhance its service management capabilities. The company aimed to standardize its ITSM processes across different geographical locations, improve service quality, and demonstrate its commitment to excellence to its customers.

The company initiated the process by setting up an ISO/IEC 20000-1 implementation team, which comprised representatives from different business units. They began by identifying and documenting the existing ITSM processes and comparing them against the ISO/IEC 20000-1 requirements.

One of the primary challenges was coordinating and standardizing processes across multiple locations with differing local practices. To tackle this, the implementation team developed a unified service management system with clear documentation of all processes and procedures.

To ensure a smooth transition, the company conducted extensive training sessions for its employees, emphasizing the benefits and importance of ISO/IEC 20000-1. They also utilized various communication channels to keep all stakeholders informed about the progress.

After rigorous efforts and stringent internal and external audits, the company achieved ISO/IEC 20000-1 certification. The certification led to significant improvements in service delivery consistency across all locations, better incident and problem management, and increased customer satisfaction. It also gave the company a competitive edge in the market, enhancing its reputation among clients and prospects.

These case studies demonstrate the transformative power of ISO/IEC 20000-1 when it's implemented correctly. Regardless of industry or size, any organization can benefit from adopting this standard, as it offers a proven framework for delivering consistent, high-quality IT services. By understanding these success stories, organizations can draw inspiration and practical insights for their own ISO/IEC 20000-1 journey.

Glossary of Key Terms and Acronyms

1. IT Service Management (ITSM): This is a strategic approach to designing, delivering, managing, and improving the way information technology (IT) is used within an organization. The goal of ITSM is to ensure that the right processes, people, and technology are in place so that the organization can meet its business goals.

2. ISO/IEC 20000-1: It's an international standard for ITSM. The standard describes a set of management processes designed to help organizations deliver more effective IT services. ISO/IEC 20000-1 was first released in 2005, and it was revised in 2011 and 2018.

3. Service Management System (SMS): It refers to the coordinated system of processes, procedures, specific policies, and activities that organizations use to implement, manage, and monitor IT services. SMS is a crucial part of the ISO/IEC 20000-1 standard.

4. IT Infrastructure Library (ITIL): ITIL is a framework of best practices for delivering IT services. It helps organizations to align IT services with their needs. ITIL is widely accepted as a standard in IT service management.

5. Service Level Agreement (SLA): An SLA is a contract or agreement between a service provider and a client that details the nature, quality, and scope of the service to be provided.

6. Continual Service Improvement (CSI): CSI is a part of the ITSM and ISO/IEC 20000-1 that focuses on continually improving IT service provision, ensuring the service provider can keep pace with increasing business demands and expectations.

7. Control Objectives for Information and Related Technologies (COBIT): COBIT is a framework created by ISACA for IT management and IT governance. It's a supporting toolset that allows managers to bridge the gap between control requirements, technical issues, and business risks.

8. Service Integration and Management (SIAM): SIAM is an approach to managing multiple suppliers of services and integrating them to provide a single business-facing IT organization.

9. Configuration Management Database (CMDB): A CMDB is a repository that acts as a data warehouse for IT installations. It holds data relating to a collection of IT assets and descriptive relationships between such assets.

10. Key Performance Indicators (KPIs): KPIs are a type of performance measurement. They evaluate the success of an organization or a particular activity in which it engages.

11. Incident Management: This is the process used by organizations to address any interruption to IT services. The primary goal is to restore normal service operations as quickly as possible to minimize the impact on business operations.

12. Problem Management: This process manages the lifecycle of all problems. The primary objectives are to prevent incidents from happening and to minimize the impact of incidents that cannot be prevented.

13. Change Management: Change management ensures standard methods and procedures are used for efficient and prompt handling of all changes to control IT infrastructure in order to minimize the number and impact of any related incidents upon service.

14. Digital Transformation: This is the integration of digital technology into all areas of a business, fundamentally changing how you operate and deliver value to customers. It's also a cultural change that requires organizations to continually challenge the status quo, experiment, and get comfortable with failure.

15. Agile: Agile is a project management and product development approach that encourages frequent inspection and adaptation, a leadership philosophy that encourages teamwork, self-organization, and accountability, and a set of engineering best practices intended to allow for the rapid delivery of high-quality software.

16. DevOps: DevOps is a set of practices that combines software development and IT operations. It aims to shorten the systems development life cycle and provide continuous delivery with high software quality.

17. Cloud Computing: Cloud computing is the on-demand availability of computer system resources, especially data storage and computing power, without direct active management by the user.

18. Artificial Intelligence (AI): AI is intelligence demonstrated by machines, unlike the natural intelligence displayed by humans and animals, which involves consciousness and emotionality. The distinction between the former and the latter categories is often revealed by the acronym chosen. 'Strong' AI is usually labeled as AGI (Artificial General Intelligence), while attempts to emulate 'natural' intelligence have been called ABI (Artificial Biological Intelligence).

The glossary provides a quick reference for key terms and acronyms relevant to IT service management and the ISO/IEC 20000-1 standard. It can be instrumental in understanding the complex language of ITSM and in communicating effectively with other IT professionals

About the author

Kris Hermans is the founder and managing director of Cybellium Ltd.

Kris is a senior cyber security consultant with 26 years of highly proficient IT and innovation experience, mainly in secure infrastructure software development, automation, integration and virtualisation, IT services, and IT management.

In 2004, Kris invented a new 3-tier remote access technology and deployed it for the enterprise market on a global scale achieving the highest level of enterprise market impact and innovation acknowledgment by Microsoft.

For the past 20 years, Kris deployed and/or managed every aspect and function of information and cyber security in the private and public sectors covering a wide variety such as:

- National and international banks
- National and European governments
- Medium and large to global enterprises covering leading financial, security, consulting, manufacturing, and IT industries.
- Microsoft, HP, IBM, Computacenter, G4S, ...

Visit www.cybellium.com for more books about this author.

Printed in Great Britain
by Amazon